CAMBRIDGE LIBRARY COLLECTION

Books of enduring scholarly value

Maritime Exploration

This series includes accounts, by eye-witnesses and contemporaries, of voyages by Europeans to the Americas, Asia, Australasia and the Pacific during the colonial period. Driven by the military and commercial interests of powers including Britain, France and the Netherlands, particularly the East India Companies, these expeditions brought back a wealth of information on climate, natural resources, topography, and distant civilisations. Their detailed observations provide fascinating historical data for climatologists, ecologists and anthropologists, and the accounts of the mariners' experiences on their long and dangerous voyages are full of human interest.

A Voyage to the South-Seas, in the Years 1740–1

The tale of the ill-fated H.M.S. *Wager* gripped the public's imagination, feeding its taste for dramatic accounts of survival against the odds. Part of George Anson's squadron that had been sent to harass Spanish ships in the Pacific, she was wrecked after rounding Cape Horn in 1741. The majority of the survivors, led by ship's gunner John Bulkeley, mutinied against their irascible and unpredictable captain and chose to make their own way home in what would become one of the most hazardous journeys ever recorded. Their journey took them over 2,000 miles in an open boat through ferocious seas, enduring starvation and extreme privation. Two years after the disaster, the thirty remaining men arrived back in England. Bulkeley and ship's carpenter John Cummins published this account in 1743. Also reissued in this series is the 1768 account of John Byron, who had been midshipman aboard the *Wager*.

Cambridge University Press has long been a pioneer in the reissuing of out-of-print titles from its own backlist, producing digital reprints of books that are still sought after by scholars and students but could not be reprinted economically using traditional technology. The Cambridge Library Collection extends this activity to a wider range of books which are still of importance to researchers and professionals, either for the source material they contain, or as landmarks in the history of their academic discipline.

Drawing from the world-renowned collections in the Cambridge University Library and other partner libraries, and guided by the advice of experts in each subject area, Cambridge University Press is using state-of-the-art scanning machines in its own Printing House to capture the content of each book selected for inclusion. The files are processed to give a consistently clear, crisp image, and the books finished to the high quality standard for which the Press is recognised around the world. The latest print-on-demand technology ensures that the books will remain available indefinitely, and that orders for single or multiple copies can quickly be supplied.

The Cambridge Library Collection brings back to life books of enduring scholarly value (including out-of-copyright works originally issued by other publishers) across a wide range of disciplines in the humanities and social sciences and in science and technology.

A Voyage to the South-Seas, in the Years 1740–1

*Containing a Faithful Narrative of the Loss
of His Majesty's Ship the Wager on a Desolate Island*

JOHN BULKELEY AND JOHN CUMMINS

CAMBRIDGE
UNIVERSITY PRESS

CAMBRIDGE
UNIVERSITY PRESS

University Printing House, Cambridge, CB2 8BS, United Kingdom

Cambridge University Press is part of the University of Cambridge.
It furthers the University's mission by disseminating knowledge in the pursuit of
education, learning and research at the highest international levels of excellence.

www.cambridge.org
Information on this title: www.cambridge.org/9781108083416

This edition first published 1743
This digitally printed version 2015

ISBN 978-1-108-08341-6 Paperback

A

VOYAGE

TO THE

SOUTH-SEAS,

In the YEARS 1740-1.

CONTAINING,

A faithful NARRATIVE of the Lofs of his Majefty's
Ship the *WAGER* on a defolate Ifland in the Latitude 47
South, Longitude 81 : 40 Weft : With the Proceedings and
Conduct of the Officers and Crew, and the Hardfhips they endured in the faid Ifland for the Space of five. Months ; their
bold Attempt for Liberty, in Coafting the Southern Part of
the vaft Region of *Patagonia*; fetting out with upwards of
Eighty Souls in their Boats ; the Lois of the Cutter ; their
Paffage through the Streights of *Magellan* ; an Account of
their Manner of living in the Voyage on Seals, Wild Horfes,
Dogs, &c. and the incredible Hardfhips they frequently un-
derwent for Want of Food of any Kind ; a Defcription of
the feveral Places where they touch'd in the Streights of
Magellan, with an Account of the Inhabitants, &c. and their
fafe Arrival to the *Brazil*, after failing one thoufand Leagues
in a Long-Boat ; their Reception from the *Portuguefe* ; an
Account of the Difturbances at *Rio Grand* ; their Arrival at
Rio Janeiro ; their Paffage and Ufage on Board a *Portuguefe*
Ship to *Lifbon* ; and their Return to *England*.

Interfperfed with many entertaining and curious Obfervations,
not taken Notice of by Sir *John Narborough*, or any other
Journalift.

The Whole compiled by Perfons concerned in the Facts related,

VIZ.

John Bulkeley and *John Cummins,*
Late Gunner and Carpenter of the WAGER.

Bold were the Men who on the Ocean firft
Spread the new Sails, when Ship-wreck was the worft :
More Dangers Now from MAN alone we find,
Than from the Rocks, the Billows, and the Wind.   WALLER.

LONDON:
Printed for JACOB ROBINSON, Publifher, at the *Golden-Lion* in *Ludgate-
Street.* M.DCC.XLIII.
[Price Bound Three Shillings and Six-pence.]

To the HONOURABLE

Edward Vernon, Efq;

Vice-Admiral of the BLUE, &c.

S I R,

WE have prefum'd to put the following Sheets under your Protection, tho' we have not the Honour of being perfonally known to you, nor have applied to you

for

for the Liberty of ufing your celebrated Name on this Occafion.

As this Book is a faithful Extract from the Journals of two *Britifh* Seamen, late Officers in his Majefty's Navy, we thought we could not more properly dedicate it than to a BRITISH ADMIRAL.

We know your Deteftation of Flattery ; and you know, from long Experience, that a *Britifh* Seaman hath a Spirit too brave to ftoop to fo degenerate a Practice.

The

The following Pages we hope will recommend themſelves to you, becauſe they are written in a plain maritime Stile, and void of Partiality and Prejudice.

The Diſtreſſes mention'd in this Book have perhaps not been equal'd in our Age; and we queſtion whether any Navigators living have, for ſo long a Continuance, ſuffer'd ſuch Variety of Hardſhips, as the unfortunate People of the *Wager*.

After ſurviving the Loſs of the Ship, and combating with Famine and innumerable Difficulties,

culties, a Remnant of us are return'd to our Native Country; but even here we are ftill unfortunate, deftitute of Employment, almoft without Support, or any Profpect of being reftor'd to our Stations, till fome important Queftions are decided, which cannot be cleared up till the Arrival of our late Captain, or at leaft the Commodore.

We, SIR, who prefent you with this Book, have been feveral Years in the Navy, and thought ourfelves well acquainted with its Laws and Difcipline,

and

and have many Certificates to produce, that we have always acted in Obedience to Command; but the Proceedings of the Officers and People, since the Loſs of the Ship, are reckon'd ſo dark and intricate, that we know not what to expect, nor what will be the Reſult of our Superiors Determination.

The only Conſolation, we have in our preſent Anxiety, is placed in a Confidence of the unbiaſs'd Integrity, Juſtice, and Humanity of the Right Honourable Perſons who will one

Day

Day determine for or againſt us.

When you read our Account of the Affair, you'll find the Facts impartially related, the whole Narrative written without the leaſt Shadow of Prejudice or Malice, and no more in Favour of ourſelves, than of the other Officers concern'd : We ſtand or fall by the Truth; if Truth will not ſupport us, nothing can.

In our Voyage from the *Brazil* to *Liſbon*, we were oblig'd to you for the generous Treatment we met with from an Enemy,

Enemy, a Subject of *Spain*, a Person of Distinction, and a Passenger in the same Ship : Your Virtues have procur'd you the Esteem even of your Enemies.

Your Zeal for the National Service deserves the Love of every *Honest Briton :* To leave an abundant Fortune, your Family, and your Country, to hazard your Life in the most perilous Expeditions, with no other Motive than to retrieve the Honour of the Nation, shows the Spirit of a true *British* Hero, and deserves the highest Commendations.

That

x   DEDICATION.

That you, SIR, may never deviate from your Integrity, but continue a Terror to the Enemies of *Britain*, an Honour to his Majefty's Service, and an Ornament to your Country, are the fincere Wifhes of,

HONOURABLE SIR,

Your moft dutiful,

And moft obedient

Humble Servants,

JOHN BULKELEY,
JOHN CUMMINS.

THE

PREFACE.

S an Introduction, we think proper to acquaint the Reader with our Reasons for causing the following Sheets to be made publick to the World. The chief Motive, which induced us to this Task, was to clear our Characters, which have been exceedingly blemish'd by Persons who (next to Heaven) owe the Preservation of their Lives to our Skill, and indefatigable Care; and who having an Opportunity of arriving before us in England,

have

have endeavour'd to raise their Repu-
tation on the Ruin of Our's.

It will appear to the Reader, on
Perusal of the following Pages, that
this Journal was attempted to be
taken from us by Violence at Rio
Janeiro ; *that we have preserved it,*
at the Hazard of our Lives ; that
there was no Journal kept after the
Loss of the Ship, by any Officers but
ourselves ; and if we had not been
careful in making Remarks on each
Day's Transactions, Persons must have
continued in the Dark, in relation
to all the subsequent Proceedings.

It is a very usual Thing to publish
Voyages, especially when the Navi-
gators have met with any extraordi-
nary Events. We believe, our Expedi-
tion, though it was not a Secret, is
allowed to be an extraordinary One,
and

*and consequently attended with ex-
traordinary Events: Indeed while the
Commodore was with us, every thing
went well, but when the Squadron se-
parated, Things began to have a
new Face; after the Loss of the* Wager,
*there was a general Disorder and Con-
fusion among the People, who were now
no longer implicitly obedient. There
were two Seamen particularly, who
propagated this Confusion, they said
they had suffer'd Ship-wreck in his
Majesty's Ship the* Biddeford, *and received no Wages from the Day that
the Ship was lost; that when they
were out of Pay, they look'd upon themselves as their own Masters, and no
longer subjected to Command. The
People however were not altogether
infected, but still continued to pay a
dutiful Respect to their Commander;
but when the Captain had rashly shot
Mr.*

Mr. Cozens (*whoſe Fate the Reader
will find particularly related*) *they
then grew very turbulent and unruly,
the Captain daily loſt the Love of the
Men, who with their Affection loſt
their Duty.*

*Our confining the Captain is reckoned
an audacious and unprecedented Action,
and our not bringing him home with
us, is reckon d worſe; but the Reader
will find that Neceſſity alſolutely compell'd us to act as we did, and that
we had ſufficient Reaſons for leaving
him behind.*

*Our Attempt for Liberty in ſailing
to the Southward through the Stroights
of* Magellan *with ſuch a number of
People, ſtow'd in a Long Boat, has been
cenſur'd as a mad Undertaking : Deſperate Diſeaſes require deſperate Re-
medies; had we gone to the Northward,
there*

there appear'd no Probability of escaping the Spaniards, *and when we had fallen into their Hands, 'tis not unlikely but they might have employed us as Drudges in their Mines for Life, therefore we rather chose to encounter all Difficulties than to become Slaves to a merciless Enemy.*

Some Persons have objected against our Capacity for keeping a Journal of this Nature; but several Judges of Maritime Affairs, allow this Work to be exact and regular. We think, Persons with a common Share of Understanding are capable of committing to Paper daily Remarks of Matters worthy their Observation, especially of Facts in which they themselves had so large a Share. We only relate such Things as could not possibly escape our Knowledge, and what we actually know

know to be true. We don't set up for Naturalists and Men of great Learning, therefore have avoided meddling with Things above our Capacity

We are also condemn'd by many for being too busy and active for Persons in our Stations. There was a Necessity for Action, and a great deal of it too; and had we been as indolent and regardless for the Preservation of the People, as others who were superior in Command, there would not have been a single Man, who was shipwreck'd in the Wager, *now in* England *to give any Relation of the Matter.*

The Gentleman who commanded in the Long-Boat on his Arrival before us at Lisbon, *represented us to the* English *Merchants in a very vile Light,*

Light, we were even advised by some of our Friends there not to return to our Country, lest we should suffer Death for Mutiny. But when the Gentlemen of the Factory had perus d our Journal, they found, if there was any Mutiny in the Case, the very Person who accused us, was the Ringleader and chief Mutineer. We were confident of our own Innocence, and determin'd to see our Country at all Events, being positive that we have acted to the best of our Under-standings, in all Respects, for the pre-servation of our Lives and Liberties ; and when our Superiors shall think proper to call us to an Account, which we expect will be at the Commodore s Arrival, we do not doubt but we shall clear ourselves in spite of all invidious Reflections and malicious Imputa-tions.

It has been hinted to us, as if publishing this Journal would give Offence to some Persons of Distinction. We can't conceive, how any Transactions relating to the Wager, *although made ever so publick, can give Offence to any Great Man at Home. Can it be any Offence to tell the World that we were ship-wreck'd in the* Wager, *when all People know it already? Don't they know that the* Wager *was one of his Majesty's Store-Ships? That we had on Board not only Naval Stores, but other Kind of Stores of an immense Value? Don't they also know that we went* Abroad *with Hopes of acquiring great Riches, but are return'd Home as poor as Beggars? We are guilty of no indecent Reproaches, or unmannerly Reflexions; though, it is certain, we cannot but lament our being engaged*
in

in so fatal an Expedition. When Persons have surmounted great Difficulties, it is a Pleasure for them to relate their Story; and if we give ourselves this Satisfaction, who has any Cause to be offended? Are we, who have faced Death in so many Shapes, to be intimidated, left we should give Offence to the — Lord knows whom? We never saw a satyrical Journal in our Lives, and we thought that Kind of Writing was the most obnoxious to give Offence.

It has been a Thing usual, in publishing of Voyages, to introduce Abundance of Fiction; and some Authors have been esteem'd merely for being marvellous. We have taken Care to deviate from those, by having a strict Regard to Truth. There are undoubtedly in this Book some Things which

which will appear incredible.   The Account we give of the Patagonian Indians, *and our own Diftreffes, tho' ever fo well attefted, will not eafily obtain Credit; and People will hardly believe that Human Nature could poffibly fupport the Miferies that we have endured.*

All the Difficulties related we have actually endur'd, and perhaps muft endure more : Till the Commodore's Arrival we cannot know our Fate; at prefent we are out of all Employment, and have nothing to fupport ourfelves and Families, but the Profits arifing from the Sale of our Journal ; which perhaps may be the Sum Total we fhall ever receive for our Voyage to the South-Seas.

A
VOYAGE
TO THE
SOUTH SEAS.

O N *Thursday* the 18th of *September* 1740, failed from St. *Hellens* his Majefty's Ship *Centurion,* Commodore *Anfon,* with the *Gloucefter, Pearl, Severn, Wager,* and *Tryal,* and two Store-fhips; this Squadron was defign'd round *Cape Horn* into the *South Seas,* to diftrefs the *Spaniards* in thofe Parts. The Ships were all in prime Order, all lately rebuilt. The Men were elevated with Hopes of growing immenfely rich, and in a few Years of returning to *Old England* loaden with the Wealth of their Enemies.

B   *Saturday*

Saturday the 20th, the *Ram-head* bearing N. by W. half W. diftant four Leagues, the Commodore hoifted his broad Pendant, and was faluted by every Ship in the Squadron, with thirteen Guns each. This Day join'd Company with us his Majefty's Ships, *Dragon, Winchefter, Chatham, South-Sea-Caftle,* and *Rye Galley,* with a large Convoy of Merchant-fhips.

Thurfday the 25th, we parted Company with the *Winchefter* and the *South-Sea-Caftle,* with their Convoys, bound for *America.*

On *Monday,* we parted Company with the *Streights* and *Turky* Convoys.

Friday, October the 3d, at Eight in the Morning, we faw two Brigantines to the South Eaft; the Commodore gave a Signal to chace; at Nine fired two Shot to bring 'em to; at Ten fpoke with the Chace, being two Brigs from *Lifbon,* bound for *New York.*

Sunday the 26th, about Five in the Morning, the *Severn* fhowed Lights, and fired feveral Guns a-head; foon after we faw the Land bearing W. by S. and at Noon the Eaft End of *Madeira* bore North, diftant five Leagues.

Wednefday we moored in *Fonchiale* Road, fo called from a City of that Name, which

is

is the Metropolis of the Ifland of *Madeira*; here we employ'd moft of our Time in getting aboard Water, and ftowing our dry Provifions between Decks.

Tuefday, November the 4th, Captain *Kidd* our Commander was removed on Board the *Pearl,* and the Honourable Captain *Murray* fucceeded him in the *Wager.* Captain *Norris* of the *Gloucefter* having obtained Leave to return to *England,* on Account of his ill State of Health, occafioned the above Removals.

While we lay at *Madeira,* we were informed of ten Sail of Ships cruifing off and on, to the Weftward; thefe Ships were judg'd to be *French,* and had been feen every Day for a Week before our Arrival: The Commodore fent out a Privateer Sloop, but fhe returned the Day following, without feeing 'em; fo that we can give no Account of 'em.

On *Wednefday* the 5th, we failed from *Madeira.* On the 20th the *Induftry* Store-fhip parted Company; and on *Friday* the 28th, by Account, we crofs'd the *Equinoctial.*

On the 17th of *December* we faw the Ifland of St. *Catharine,* at Noon; the Northmoft Land in Sight bore W. N. W. and the Southmoft S. W. by W. Variation *per* Amplitude 13 : 57 Eafterly.

On

On the 18th, the North End of the Ifland of St. *Catharine* bore N.W. by W. diftant feven Leagues; and the Ifland of *Gaul* bore N. W. diftant fix Leagues.

On the 19th we anchor'd in St. *Catharine*'s Bay, in upward of twelve Fathom Water, the Ifland *Gaul* on the Coaft of *Brazil* bearing N. by E. diftant four Leagues. On the 20th we anchor'd in St. *Catharine*'s Road, and the Day following we moored between the Ifland of St. *Catharine* and the *Main*.

On *Monday* the 22d, the Commodore ordered frefh Beef for the fick People.

On the 27th came in a *Portuguefe* Brig from *Rio Janeiro*, for the *Rio Grand*: While we lay here, the People were generally employ'd in over-hauling the Rigging, and getting aboard Water.

On the 17th of *January* 1741, we failed from St. *Catharine*'s; the Commodore faluted the Fort with eleven Guns, the Fort returned the fame Number.

On *Thurfday* the 22d we loft Sight of the *Pearl*.

On *Tuefday* the 17th of *February*, the *Pearl* join'd the Squadron; and on the 19th we came to Anchor off the River of St. *Julian*'s, on the Coaft of *Patagonia*, St. *Julian*'s Hill

Hill bearing S. W. by W. and the Southmoſt
Land in Sight S. by E. diſtant from the Shore
three Leagues. This Day our Captain, the
Honourable *George Murray*, took Command
on Board the *Pearl*, Captain *Kidd* having
died on the Voyage ſince we left St. *Catharine's.*

Captain *Kidd* was heard to ſay, a few
Days before his Death, That this Voyage,
which both Officers and Sailors had engag'd
in, with ſo much Cheerfulneſs and Alacrity,
would prove in the End very far from their
Expeƈtations, notwithſtanding the vaſt Trea-
ſure they imagined to gain by it; that it
would end in Poverty, Vermin, Famine,
Death, and Deſtruƈtion. How far the Captain's Words were prophetick, will appear in
the Courſe of our Journal. Captain *C——p*
ſucceeded Captain *Murray* on Board the
Wager.

On the 26th of *February* we ſent on Board
the *Pearl* twelve Butts and two Puncheons
of Water; the *Pearl* having, while ſhe was
ſeparated from us, been chaſed by five large
Spaniſh Men of War, the Commander in Chief
being diſtinguiſh'd by a red broad *Pendant*
with a Swallow's Tail at his Main-top-maſt
Head, and a red Flag at his Enſign-ſtaff:
During

During the Chace, the *Pearl,* in order to clear Ship, threw over-board and ftove fourteen Tons of Water; fhe likewife ftove the Long-Boat, and threw her over-board, with Oars, Sails and Booms, and made all clear for engaging; but Night coming on, at Seven o' Clock loft Sight of the Enemy; at Five in the Morning faw the *Spanifh* Ships from the Maft-head, two Points on the Lee-quarter, ftill giving Chace, and crowding all the Sail they could; but at Nine the *Pearl* loft Sight of 'em entirely. We judged this to be Admiral *Pizarro's* Squadron, fent out in Purfuit of Commodore *Anfon.* Had our Ships united fallen in with 'em, 'tis probable we might have given a good Account of 'em. While we lay at St. *Julian's,* we faw the Sea full of Shrimps, and red as if they were boiled; the Water appeared tinftured to that Degree, that it look'd like Blood.

On the 27th, we fent on Board the *Pearl* four Puncheons of Water more; at Six in the Morning, the Commodore made Signal to weigh; at Eight weigh'd, and came to Sail; this Day we loft Sight of the *Gloucefter.*

The 28th, the *Gloucefter* came into the Squadron again.

On the 7th of *March* we pafs'd through the Streights of *Le Mair*; Cape *Diego* on the Ifland of *Terra del Fuego* bore N. W. by W. three Leagues, and the Weft End of the Ifland, Staten Land, bore E. N. E. diftant Four Leagues, the Squadron under Reeft Courfes.

On the 10th we loft Sight of the *Ann* Pink, on the 12th carried away the Rails and Timbers of the Head on both Sides.

On the 16th the *Ann* Pink join'd the Squadron again.

The 30th the *Gloucefter* broke her Main-Yard in the Slings.

April the 1ft, the Commodore order'd Mr. *Cummins*, the Carpenter, on Board the *Gloucefter*.

On the 8th carried away the Mizen-Maft, two Feet above the Awning; there was no Sail on the Maft. Upon the Rowl of a Sea, all the Chain-Plates to Wind-ward broke, Lat. 56. 31. Long. 87. 4 Weft. At Noon Cape St. *Bartholomew* bore North, 84 Deg. E. diftant 229 Leagues.

The 10th loft Sight of the *Severn* and *Pearl*, Lat. 56. 29. Long. 85 Weft. At Ten laft Night fell in with two fmall Iflands; at Eight in the Morning the Iflands bore N.N.W. by the Compafs diftant eight Leagues, in the

Latitude

Latitude 54. 00 South; we took 'em for the Iflands which lay off *Brewer's Streights*, Latitude 54 : 50 South, Long. 84. 56 Weft.

On the 12th we had very hard Gales at Weft, with the largeft Swell I ever faw; I was Officer of the Watch (tho' I was Gunner of the Ship, I had the Charge of a Watch during the whole Voyage); we had our Larboard Tacks on Board : Between Six and Seven in the Morning, holding by the Topfail Hallyards to Wind-ward, there broke a Sea in the Ship, which carried me over the Wheel, bilg'd the Cutter, and canted her off the Skeet's Bottom up athwart the Barge; it likewife half filled the Long-Boat; the Boatfwain was for heaving the Cutter over-board, I order'd him to do nothing with her till I had acquainted the Captain, who was then very ill in his Cabbin : The Captain defired me to ufe all Means to fave the Cutter; at the fame Time I asked Leave to skuttle the Long-Boat, and get the Sprit-fail Yard and Jib in, for fear of endangering the Bowfprit; which he ordered to be done, and told me, It was a very great Misfortune that he fhould be ill at fuch a Time. When I came from the Captain, I found the Lieutenant on the Deck, got the Cutter in her Place, skuttled the

the Long-Boat, and got the Sprit-fail Yard and Jib-boom in. The Carpenter is still aboard the *Gloucefter*.

The 13th, under Reeft Courfes, the Larboard Tacks; the Commodore being on the Weather-Quarter, bore down under our Lee, and fpoke with us. He ask'd the Captain, If the Carpenter was return'd from the *Gloucefter?* The Captain anfwer'd, No; and am furprized Capt. *M——ll* fhould detain him, when he knows I muft want him about my Mizen-Maft. The Commodore told him he would fpeak with the *Gloucefter*, and order him on Board. He then ask'd the Captain, Why he did not fet the Main-top-fail, and make more Sail? Capt. *C——p* made Anfwer, My Rigging is all gone, and broke fore and aft, and my People almoft all taken ill, and down; but I will fet him as foon as poffible. The Commodore defired he would, and make what Sail he could after him.

The 14th, the Carpenter return'd from the *Gloucefter*, it being the only Day this Fortnight a Boat could live in the Sea. As foon as the Carpenter came on Board, he waited on the Captain, who order'd him to look on the Chain-Plates and Chains, and to give his Opinion cf the Maft's going away. The

C   Car.

Carpenter look'd as order'd, and gave Capt. C—p for Anſwer, That the Chain-Plates were all broke. The Captain ſhook his Head, and ſaid, Carpenter! that is not the Reaſon of the Maſt's going away. The Carpenter, not willing, as the Maſt was gone, to lay it to any one's Miſmanagement, or to occaſion any Uneaſineſs about what was now paſt Prevention, fitted a Capp on the Stump of the Mizen-Maſt, got up a lower Studding-Sail-Boom of 40 Feet, and hoiſted a Sail to keep the Ship to.

To-day, being the 19th, and the fineſt Day we had in theſe Seas, we were employ'd in repairing the Rigging; we bent a new Main-Sail and Reeft him, as did the *Anne* Pink; the *Glouceſter* at the ſame Time fix'd her Main-Yard; the Commodore and *Tryal* keeping a-head, and at a conſiderable Diſtance; between Four and Six at Night ſaw the Commodore's Light. At Six, being reliev'd by the Maſter, he could not ſee the Commodore's Light, tho' it was viſible to every one elſe on the Quarter-Deck: The Maſter ſtill perſiſted he could not ſee it; on which I went and acquainted the Captain, who came upon Deck, and ſeeing the Light, ask'd the Maſter, Where his Eyes were? This was the laſt

Time

Time I ever faw the Commodore. The Lieutenant having the firft Watch loft Sight of him at Nine o' Clock, and at Ten was oblig'd to hand the Fore-Sail; in doing of which we loft a Seaman over-board. We faw the *Gloucefter* and *Anne* Pink a-ftern in the Morning; but they were foon gone a-head, and out of Sight.

The 21ft, as I was in the Steward's Room, *Jofeph King*, Seaman, came for a Pound of Bread. I heard him ask the Steward, If he thought they would be ferv'd with the fame Quantity of Water as before? Without waiting for an Anfwer, No, G – d d — n 'em; as the Commodore was parted, they fhould find the Difference. Not knowing the Confequence of this, or by whom the Fellow might be fpirited up, I acquainted the Captain with the Affair, who order'd me to deliver a Brace of Piftols charg'd with a Brace of Balls to every Officer in the Ship who wanted 'em, and to take no farther Notice of the Matter.

May the 1ft. This Day the Officers were call'd, and their Opinions ask'd concerning the beft Bower-Anchor; refolv'd to cut the Anchor away, for fear of endangering the Ship, there being no Poffibility of fecuring it without putting our Fore-Maft in extreme Danger, the Shrouds and Chain-Plates being all broke.

Fourteen Days before the Lofs of the Ship, the Wind at S. and S. S. W. fteer'd N. W. by N. and N. N, W. by the Compafs: Laid the Ship to for the firft four Nights; the meaning of this I could not learn. I ask'd the Lieutenant the Reafon of our bearing for the Land on a Lee-Shore, when we had a fair Wind for our Rendezvous, which I had always thought was for the Ifland of *Juan Ferdinandez.* The Lieutenant told me the Rendezvous was alter'd to an Ifland in the Latitude of 44 : S. Upon this I faid to the Lieutenant, This is a very great Misfortune to us; that we can do nothing with the Ship in the Condition fhe is in upon a Lee-fhore; and am furpriz'd, that we fhould be oblig'd to go there. The Lieutenant told me, he had faid every Thing he could to diffuade the Captain from it, but found him determin'd to go there. The fifth Night, and every Night after, made Sail; the Wind to the Weftward. I never reliev'd the Lieutenant, but I ask'd him, What he thought of a Lee-fhore with the Ship in this Condition? He always reply'd, He could not tell. We

saw

faw Rock-weed in abundance pafs by the
Ship. The Honourable *J——n B——n,*
Midfhipman, being on the Quarter-Deck,
faid, We can't be far off the Land by thefe
Weeds. The Lieutenant and Mate being by,
I faid, Gentlemen, What can we do with the
Ship in the miferable Condition fhe is in on a
Lee-fhore? The Lieutenant anfwer'd, Whenever I have been with the Captain fince our
firft lying to, I always perfuaded him to go
for *Juan Ferdinandez*; therefore I would
have you go to him, he may be perfuaded
by you, tho' he will not by me. I faid, If
that was the Cafe, my going to him is need-
lefs. In a Quarter of an Hour afterwards, the
Captain fent for me, and faid, Gunner! What
Longitude have you made? I told him 82:
30. What Diftance do you reckon yourfelf
off the Land? I anfwer'd, About 60 Leagues:
But if the two Iflands we faw are thofe which
are laid down in your Chart to lay off *Brewer's
Streights,* and the fame Current continues
with the Weftern Swell, we can't be above
a third Part of the Diftance off the Land.
The Captain made Anfwer, As for the Cur-
rents, there is no Account to be given for
'em; fometimes they fet one Way, and fometimes another. I faid, Sir, very true; but

as

as the Ship has been always under Reeft Courfes, with the Mizen-Maft gone, fhe muft wholly drive to Leeward, and nigher the Land than expe&ed. The Captain then told me, I fupppofe you are not unacquainted of my Rendezvous for the Ifland of *Noftra Signora Di Socora*, in the Latitude of 44. I reply'd, Sir, the Ship is in a very bad Condition to come in with the Lee-fhore; and if it is poffible to bring the Ship to an Anchor, we fhall never purchafe him again. The Captain anfwer'd, I don't defign to come to an Anchor; for there are no Soundings until you come within feven Leagues of the Land. I purpofe to ftand off and on twenty-four Hours; and if I don't fee the Commodore, or any of the Squadron in that Time, we will go for *Juan Ferdinandez*. To this I faid, Sir, the Ship is a perfe&t Wreck; our Mizen-Maft gone, with our ftanding Rigging afore and abaft, and all our People down; therefore I can't fee what we can do in with the Land. The Captain's Anfwer was, It does not fignify, I am oblig'd and determin'd to go for the firft Rendezvous.

On the 13th, at Eight in the Morning, the Straps of the Fore-Jeer Blocks broke; reev'd the Top Ropes, and lower'd the Yard; went

to

to ftrapping the Blocks. At Nine, the Carpenter going forward to infpeƈt the Chain-Plates, faw the Land from the Fore-caftle; on which he ask'd the Boatfwain's Mate, who was by him, If he faw the Land? He anfwer'd, No. The Carpenter fhew'd it him, and he faw it plain. The Carpenter then fhew'd it to the Lieutenant; but he would not believe it to be Land, becaufe it bore N. N. W. and faid it was impoffible; there-fore he never inform'd the Captain of the Sight of Land, as the Honourable Mr. *B—n* hath heard the Captain fay. At Two in the Afternoon lower'd the Fore-yard, and hawl'd the Fore-fail up. Notwithftanding I was Officer of the Watch, I was oblig'd to go upon the Fore-yard, where was Mr. *Camp-bell* Midfhipman, one Boatfwain's Mate, four Seamen, and the Mafter's Servant; which were all the Hands we could get out of the Ship's Company to affift. Whilft on the Yard I faw the Land very plain, on the Lar-board-beam bearing N. W. half N. neareft High Land, with Hillocks, and one remark-able Hommacoe like a Sugar-loaf, very high. At the Sight of Land I came off the Fore-yard, and acquainted the Captain. He im-mediately gave Orders to fway the Fore-yard

up,

up, and fet the Fore-fail; then we wore Ship with her Head to the Southward. The Captain coming forward unhappily received a Fall, which diflocated his Shoulder, fo that he was obliged to be put into the Surgeon's Cabbin. Some Time after he fent for the Lieutenant and myfelf, acquainting us of the Neceffity there was for making Sail, as being on a Lee-fhore; therefore defired we would ufe our utmoft Endeavours to crowd the Ship off. You fee, Gentlemen, faid he, my Misfortune will not permit me to continue on the Deck: As for the Mafter, he is not worthy of the Charge of a Watch; therefore I muft defire you, Mr. *Bulkeley,* to be in the Watch with him, and to make but two Watches: Keep a good Look-out, and, if poffible, fet the Main-top-fail. Mr. *B——s,* I muft defire Mr. *Cummins* to be with you; and beg you will take all the Care you can. I having the firft Watch, fet the Main, Fore and Mizen Stay-fail; it blew fo hard I found it impoffible to fet the Main-top-fail; of which I acquainted the Captain: All the Hands we could mufter in both Watches, Officers included, were but twelve; the reft of the Ship's Company were all fick below: I very often could get no more than three

Seamen

Seamen in my Watch. The Ship for thefe three Weeks hath been no better than a Wreck; the Mizen-Maft gone; the ftanding Rigging and Chain-Plates, afore and abaft, moftly broke and ruin'd. The Top-fails now at the Yards are fo bad, that if we attempt to loofe 'em for making Sail, we are in Danger of fplitting 'em; and we have not a fpare Sail in the Ship that can be brought to the Yard without being repair'd. This is the prefent deplorable Situation of the Ship All the firft and middle Watch it blow'd and rain'd; and withal fo very dark, that we could not fee the Length of the Ship: For the greateft Part of the Night fhe came up no nearer than S. by W and S. S. W. At Four in the Morning fhe came up with her Head Weft; fo that her Head was then off the Shore.

Thurfday, May the 14th, 1741, at Half an Hour paft Four this Morning, the Ship ftruck abaft on a funken Rock, founded fourteen Fathom; but it being impoffible to let go the Anchor Time enough to bring her up, being furrounded on every Side with Rocks, (a very difmal Profpect to behold!) the Ship ftruck a fecond Time, which broke the Head of the Tiller; fo that we were obliged to fteer her with the Main and Fore-fheets, by

D eafing

eafing off one, and hawling aft the other, as
fhe came to, or fell off. In a fhort Time
after, fhe ftruck, bilged, and grounded, between two fmall Iflands, where Providence
directed us to fuch a Place as we could fave
our Lives. When the Ship ftruck it was
about Break of Day, and not above a Musket-
fhot from the Shore. Launch'd the Barge,
Cutter, and Yawl over the Gunnel; cut the
Main and Fore-Maft by the Board, and the
Sheet-Anchor from the Gunnel. The Captain fent the Barge afhore, with Mr. S—w the
Mate, to fee if the Place was inhabited, and
to return aboard directly; but, without any
Regard to his Duty, or the Prefervation of
the Lives of the People, he ftaid afhore.
The Barge not returning as expected, the
Lieutenant was fent in the Yawl, with
Orders to bring off the Barge. The Lieute-
nant tarried afhore, but fent off the Boat.
As foon as the Boat came on Board, the Captain, being very ill, was perfuaded by the
Officers to go afhore: With the Captain
went the Land-Officers, Mate, and Midfhipmen; the Officers remaining on Board
were the Mafter, Boatfwain, Gunner, and
Carpenter: The Boatfwain, who was laid up
a Month before the Lofs of the Ship, became

of

of a fudden very vigorous and active. At
Night it blow'd very hard at North, with a
great tumbling Sea ; we expected every Moment that the Ship would part, fetching fuch
Jirks and Twiftings as fhock'd every Perfon
aboard, who had the leaft Care for the Prefervation of Life; yet, in the difmal Situation we were in, we had feveral in the Ship
fo thoughtlefs of their Danger, fo ftupid,
and infenfible of their Mifery, that upon the
principal Officers leaving her, they fell into
the moft violent Outrage and Diforder: They
began with broaching the Wine in the Lazaretto; then to breaking open Cabbins and
Chefts, arming themfelves with Swords and
Piftols, threatning to murder thofe who fhould
oppofe or queftion them : Being drunk and
mad with Liquor, they plunder d Chefts and
Cabbins for Money and other Things of Value, cloathed themfelves in the richeft Apparel they could find, and imagined themfelves
Lords Paramount.

Friday the 15th the Ship was bilged in the
Mid-fhips on a great Rock; we took Care
to fecure fome Powder, Ball, and a little
Bread. In the Afternoon, the Carpenter and
myfelf went afhore with feveral of thofe
imaginary Lords in the rich Attire they had
plunder'd

plunder'd Yesterday; but upon the Purser and Lieutenant *Hamilton* of Marines presenting Pistols to some of their Breasts, those Grandees suffer'd themselves very quietly to be disrob'd of all their Greatness, and in a few Minutes look'd like a Parcel of transported Felons. On our coming ashore, we found the Captain had taken his Lodging in a little Hut, suppofed to be built by *Indians*; as for our Parts, we were forced to take Shelter under a great Tree, where we made a large Fire; but it rain'd so hard, that it had almoft coft us our Lives; an Invalid died that very Night on the Spot. Before I left the Ship I went to my Cabbin for my Journal, but could not find it; I believe it is destroy'd with the reft, for there is not one Journal to be produced; we have good Reason to apprehend there was a Person employ'd to deftroy them; I afterwards found Part of the Mafter's Journal along Shore, tore to Pieces: Whatever is related in this Book, preceding the Lofs of the *Wager*, is extracted from a Journal belonging to a Gentleman lately an Officer on Board the *Pearl*. After we loft Sight of the *Pearl*, I was obliged to have Recourse to my Memory, which I believe has been very faithful to me. From the

the Time we were Ship-wreck'd, the Carpenter and myfelf were exceeding careful in writing each Day's Tranfactions: Had other Perfons taken the fame Care, there would be no Neceffity of impofing upon the Publick a partial and inconfiftent Narrative, inftead of a faithful Relation of Facts.

On the 16th, the Weather very boifterous and a great Sea, the Boatfwain wanted a Boat; but finding no Appearance of any coming aboard, brought a Quarter-deck Gun, a four Pounder, to bear on the Captain's Hut, and fir'd two Shot, which went juft over the Captain's Tent. This Day, being refolv'd to contrive fomething like a Houfe, to fecure us from the Inclemency of the Rain, and Severity of the Weather, we hawl'd up the Cutter, and propping her up we made a tolerable Habitation. As for Food this Ifland produces none; nor is there any Vegetable upon it but Cellery, which grows here in abundance, and is of great Ufe to us, the Men being in general very much troubled with the Scurvy.

On the 17th of *May*, being *Whitfunday*, got feveral wild Fowls, and Plenty of Mufcles, Limpetts, and other Shel-fifh, which we find very refrefhing, having fubfifted a long Time on nothing but Salt-provifions.

The

The 18th went on Board the Ship, to fee if it was poffible to come to any Provifions; got out of the Lazaretto two Casks of Flower and fome Wine, which were very ufeful.

On the 19th went aboard again to fcuttle the Decks, in order to get fome Beef and Pork out of the Hold; we alfo fcuttled the Carpenter's Store-room, for Nails and other Things of Service.

The 20th cut away the Gunnel, to get the Long Boat out; which was done. To-day we found feveral Men dead, and fome drowned, in the Ship; fuppos'd to have drank till they were not able to get from the Water, as it flowed into the Ship. While we were aboard working on the Wreck, there came a-long-fide a Canoe with feveral *Indians*, bowing and croffing themfelves, giving us to underftand they were inclineable to the *Romifh* Religion; we gave 'em out of the Ship two Bales of Cloth, and fent them afhore to the Captain; he gave them Hats, and prefented each of them with a Soldier's Coat. They had Abundance of the largeft and beft Mufcles I ever faw, or tafted. This Day was the firft Time of the Boatfwain's coming afhore; the Captain called him Rogue and Villain, and felled him to the Ground with his Cane, fo that he

was

was motionlefs, and to Appearance dead;
when he had recovered the Blow, and faw a
cockt Piftol in the Captain's Hand, he offered
his naked Breaft; the Captain told him, he
deferved to be fhot, and faid no more to him.
The Captain, Lieutenant *H - n* of Marines, the
Surgeon, and Purfer, always appear'd in Arms
on the Beach, on the coming afhore of every
Boat, in order to prevent the People bringing
any Thing from the Ship in a clandeftine
Manner; they were fo cautious of any Thing
being imbezzled, that they would not fuffer
the Boats to go off and work by Night, notwithftanding the Moon, Tides, and Fairnefs
of Weather were more favourable to us by
Night than Day; by this we omitted feveral
Opportunities of getting out Provifions, and
other ufeful Things, which we fhall fhortly
ftand in great Need of.

The 21ft, continue to fcuttle between
Decks, in getting Neceffaries out of the Ship;
found feveral Men dead.

The 22d, the *Indians* brought us three
Sheep, and fome Mufcles. They are a People of a fmall Stature, well fhaped, of an
Olive Complexion, with black Hair; in Behaviour very civil: they have little Cloaths,
except about their Waifts, notwithftanding
the

the Climate is exceſſive cold. They ſtay'd all Night, it being very rainy Weather, and has been ever ſince we have been here, the Wind blowing from North to N. W.

Saturday the 23d, the Wind from the E. N. E. to North, fell Abundance of Snow, inſomuch that the Mountains are cover'd with it. It freezes very hard, and we find it extreamly cold. The next Day, the ſame Weather, we went aboard, and ſcuttled for Flower in the Forehold.

The 25th, little Wind at N. E. and froſty Weather, went aboard again, and got out of the Forehold eight Barrels of Flower, one Cask of Peaſe, with ſome Brandy and Wine. This Day went to Allowance, of half a Pound of Flower *per* Man, and one Piece of Pork for three Men, it being the firſt Time of ſerving ſince on Shore.

The 26th, we got out more Casks of Flower, one Cask of Oatmeal, with ſome Brandy and Wine. In the Evening the *Indians* came with their Wives, we gave the Women Hats, and the Men Breeches; they made Signs as if they would bring more Sheep.

On the 27th, we ſcuttled over the Captain's Store-room, got out ſeveral Casks of Rum and Wine, and brought them aſhore. This
was

was the firft Time of the Lieutenant's being between Decks fince the Lofs of the Ship. The following Day we went aboard, cut down and toft over-board the Ship's Awning, to make a Deck for the Long Boat.

Since the 27th, we have been employ'd in getting up the Long Boat, and repairing the Barge which had been ftove afhore. Rainy Weather.

On *Wednefday*, the 3d of *June*, hard Gales of Wind at N. N. Weft, with Abundance of Rain; deferted this Day *James Mitchel*, Carpenter's Mate, *John Ruffell*, Armourer, *William Oram*, Carpenter's Crew, *Jofeph King*, *John Redwood*, Boatfwain's Yeoman, *Dennis O'Lary*, *John Davis*, *James Roach*, *James Stewart*, and *William Thompfon*, Seamen. Took up, along Shore, one Hogfhead of Brandy, and feveral Things that drove out of the Ship, as Bales of Cloth, Hats, Shoes, and other Neceffaries. An Information was given, this Day, by *David Buckley*, to the Captain, that there was a Defign to blow him up, with the Surgeon, and Lieutenant *H———n* of Marines. The Train was actually found, laid by the Deferters, to blow 'em up the Night before they went off.

E   *Thurfday*

Thursday the 4th, we finished the Boats, and shot several wild Geese. Finding Murmurings and Discontents among the People, we secured the Oars, and hawled up the Boats, being apprehensive they would go away with them by Night.

The 5th, we went on Board the Ship, found several Casks of Wine and Brandy between Decks, most Part of the Planks between Decks gone, and some Strakes to Windward started out, Part of the upper Deck blown up, the Stumps of the Masts and Pumps risen five Feet; brought ashore one Cask of Flower, with some Stuff for the Use of the Long Boat; and two Quarter Casks of Wine; the Wind at S. by E.

Saturday the 6th, the Wind at South and fair Weather, we went aboard, got out of the Hold eight Casks of Flower, two Casks of Wine, a Quarter Cask and three Hogsheads of Brandy. The Lieutenant went to the *Indians*, but could not find 'em, being inform'd by the Deserters that they were gone.

On *Sunday* the 7th, we went aboard the Ship, got out a Cask of Pork, two Barrels of Flower, started one Pipe of Wine, and brought it ashore, with a Quarter Cask of Pease, some Bales of Cloth, and Carpenter's Stores. This

Day

Day Mr. *Henry Cozens*, Midſhipman, was confin'd by the Captain; the Fault alledg'd a-
gainſt him was Drunkenneſs. We learn from
Nicholas Griſelham, Seaman, who was preſent
and near the Captain all the Time, that as
Mr. *Cozens* was rowling up a ſteep Beach a
Cask of Peaſe, he found it too heavy for him,
and left off rowling; the Captain ſeeing this
told him, he was drunk; Mr. *Cozens* reply'd,
With what ſhould I get drunk, unleſs it be
with Water? The Captain. then ſaid, You
Scoundrel, get more Hands, and rowl the
Cask up: *Cozens* called for more Hands, but
no People came; with that the Captain ſtruck
him with hisCane. *Griſelham* likewiſe ſays,that
Cozens talked to the Captain about one Capt.
Sh—lv—k; but theWords he does notremem-
ber. But the ſame Night I heard Mr. *Cozens*
uſe very unbecoming Language to the Captain, telling him, That he was come into
thoſe Seas to pay *Sh—lv—k*'s Debts; and
alſo inſolently added, Tho' *Sh—lv—k* was a
Rogue, he was not a Fool; and, by G——d,
you are both. When he ſpoke this, he was
a Priſoner in the Store-Tent, and asked the
Captain, If he was to be kept there all Night?
On theſe Provocations, the Captain attempted
to ſtrike him again; but the Centinel ſaid,
he

he fhould ftrike no Prifoner of his. But *Co-zens* endeavouring to ftave a Cask of Brandy, was foon after releafed. This Day got out of the Ship feveral Chefts of Wax Candles of all Sizes, Bales of Cloth, Bales of Stockings, Shoes, with fome Clocks, and mercantile Wares, with which the Ship was throng'd.

The 8th, Mr. *Cummins* and myfelf went to the Deferters; we find they are determined to go off to the Northward; the Reafon of their Stay is the Want of Graft to go off in. They now find themfelves miftaken, they believed at firft they were on the Main, but are convinced they are four or five Leagues from it, therefore they purpofe to build a Punt out of the Wreck of the Ship: They live on Sea Weed and Shell Fifh; got up one Cask of Beef, which was brought on Shore with a Cask of Brandy, found one Cask of Beef on the Rocks.

On *Tuefday* the 9th, I went with the Doctor's Mate to the Deferters, and fpoke to *William Oram*, a Carpenter, and a very ufeful Man, defiring him to return, with a Promife of Pardon from the Captain: In this Affair I was obliged to act very fecretly. To-day, Mr. *Cozens*, the Midfhipman, had a Dif-pute with the Surgeon; the latter having
fome

fome Bufinefs in our Tent, which when he had done, on his going away, Mr. *Cozens* followed him; they foon fell to Blows, but the Surgeon had fo much the Advantage of the Midfhipman, that he tied his Hands behind him and left him. In the Evening the Captain fent for me and the Carpenter to his Tent: We found with the Captain, the Lieutenant, Purfer, Surgeon, and Lieutenant *H———n* of Marines. Here we had a Confultation, which was chiefly concerning the Difturbances among the People, as well in our Tent as in the reft. Mr. *Cummins* and I affured the Captain, that the People in our Tent were generally very well affected to him, and that we never would engage in any Mutiny againft him, or any other Officer that would act for the publick Good, and his Majefty's Service: The Captain faid, he had no Reafon to fufpect us, for we were the only two in the Ship, that he put any Truft or Confidence in; ftrict Orders were given the Centinel to keep a good Look-out, and have a watchful Eye on the Provifions; notwithftanding all this Precaution and Care, there was one third Part of a Barrel of Flower, and half a Barrel of Gunpowder taken away that Night. It is to be obferved, that this

Day's

Day's Confultation was the firft that Captain
C---p ever had with his Officers; had he
fometimes confulted them aboard, we might
probably have efcaped our prefent unhappy
Condition.

Wednefday the 10th, This Day, ferving
the Provifions, the Boatfwain's Servant, a
Portuguefe Boy, talking bad *Englifh*, and
bringing in the Allowance of Wine, the
Boatfwain, Mr. *Cozens* Midfhipman, and the
Cook his Meff-mates, with fome Difficulty,
underftood by the Boy's Talk, that one of
the Men had his Allowance ftopped; Mr.
Cozens went to know the Reafon; the Purfer
and he having fome Difpute two or threeDays
before, the Purfer told him, when he asked
for his Wine, that he was come to Mutiny,
and, without any farther Ceremony, dif-
charged a Piftol at his Head, and would have
fhot him, had he not been prevented by the
Cooper's canting the Piftol with his Elbow,
at the Inftant of its going off; the Captain,
and Lieutenant *H---n*, hearing the Difcharge of the Piftol, the latter ran out with
a Firelock, then called the Captain out of his
Tent, telling him that *Cozens* was come to
Mutiny; the Captain on this jumped out, asking where the Villain was, clapped a cock'd
Piftol

Piftol to Mr. *Cozens's* Cheek, and precipi-
tately fhot him, without asking any Queftions;
the Noife of the two Piftols going off, reached
our Tent; it was rainy Weather, and not
fit for Gunning, fo that we could not imagine
the Meaning of it; foon after we heard Mr.
Cozens was fhot by the Captain: The Lieutenant came to call all Hands to the Captain;
I asked if we muft go armed; the Lieutenant anfwered, yes; but, on Confideration, I
thought better to go without Arms: When
we came to the Captain, he acquainted us
with what he had done, and told us he was
ftill our Commander. The Captain, Purfer,
Surgeon, Lieutenants *H——— n, E———rs,*
and *F—— ng* of Marines being all armed, I
faid to the Captain, Sir, you fee we are
difarmed; on this the Captain dropped his
Firelock to the Ground, faying, I fee you are,
and have only fent for you, to let you all
know I am ftill your Commander, fo let every Man go to his Tent; accordingly every
Man obeyed him. In our Tent we had eighteen of the ftouteft Fellows that belonged to
the Ship; and I believe the Captain, and the
Gentlemen above-mentioned, have fome Suf-
picion of Mr. *Cummins* and myfelf, believing
we can fway moft of the Seamen on Shore:
But

But I think this Day we have given a Proof of the Sincerity of our Intentions, and our Deteftation of Mutiny, by not appearing in Arms at the Report of Mr. *Cozens* being fhot; we walked up with the Captain, where we faw Mr. *Cozens* with his Elbow on the Ground refting his right Cheek on the Palm of his Hand, alive, and to Appearance fenfible, but fpeechlefs; the Captain ordered him to the fick Tent, the Surgeon's Mate dreffed his left Cheek where he was fhot, and felt a Ball about three Inches under his right Eye; the Surgeon refufed dreffing him; this we may impute to his having lately a Quarrel with Mr. *Cozens*, which has been already mentioned. The fhooting of Mr. *Cozens* was a very unhappy Affair; the Perfon whofe Allowance was ftopped, made no Complaint to him; he was too officious in the Bufinefs, and his preceding Behaviour, and notorious difrefpeſtful Words to the Captain, might probably make the Captain fufpeſt his Defign was Mutiny; tho' this we muft aver, that Mr. *Cozens* neither on this, or any other Occafion, appeared in Arms fince the Lofs of the Ship: However, his Fate laid the Foundation of a great deal of Mifchief which afterwards followed.

Thurfday

Thurſday the 11th, moderate Gales at W.
N. W. The Carpenter employed in laying the
Blocks for the Long-Boat Dr. *O—y*, of the
Land Forces, was deſired to aſſiſt the Surgeon's Mate, to take the Ball out of Mr. *Cozens*'s Cheek, which he then was inclinable to
do; but in the Afternoon, finding it not a-
greeable to the Captain, refuſed to go, as we
are informed by the Surgeon's Mate, who
deſired ſome Surgeon might be preſent, to be
Witneſs of the Operation ; the Ball was taken
out, and for ſome time ſuppoſed to be loſt,
but was afterwards found.

This Day being the 12th, the Carpenter
finiſhed the Blocks for lengthening the Long-
Boat; in the Morning he went to the Captain's Tent for ſome Bolts for the Uſe of the
Long-Boat, where he ſaw the Surgeon at the
Medicine-Cheſt, who asked him how that
unfortunate Creature did, meaning Mr. *Cozens*; the Carpenter told him he had not ſeen
him To-day : The Surgeon then ſaid he would
have viſited him, but the Captain would not
give him Leave. This was looked on as an
Act of Inhumanity in the Captain, and con-
tributed very much to his loſing the Affec-
tions of the People, whoſe Opinion was,
that as Mr. *Cozens* was very ſtrong and heal-

F   thy,

thy, with proper Affiftance he might recover; the People did not fcruple to fay that
the Captain would act a more honourable
Part to difcharge another Piftol at him,
and difpatch him at once, than to deny him
Relief, and fuffer him to languifh in a cold
wet Place in Pain and Mifery.

On the 13th, Mr. *Cozens* being, to all out-
ward Appearance, likely to recover, defired
he might be removed to our Tent, which
was his Place of Refidence before this unhappy Accident : We being unwilling to dif-
oblige the Captain, the Carpenter and myfelf waited on him; we told him, we were
come to ask a Favour, hoping that he would
have fo much Mercy and Compaffion on the
unhappy Man who was in the fick Tent, as
to permit us to remove him to his former
Lodging; but the Captain anfwer'd, No; I
am fo far from it, that, if he lives, I will
carry him a Prifoner to the Commodore, and
hang him.

On the 14th, went aboard the Ship, but
could do nothing, fhe worling fo very much;
we brought afhore the Fore-top-fail Yard;
the Boat went up the River, brought back
Abundance of Geefe and Shaggs. Wind at
Weft.

Monday

Monday the 15th, hard Gales of Wind at Weft, with Rain and Hail; drove afhore three Barrels of Flower, and abundance of fmall Stuff out of the Ship; took up a-long Shore feveral Pieces of Pork and Beef; *John Anderfon*, a Seaman, walking round the Rocks, and reaching after a Piece of Beef, flipping his Footing, was drown'd, but taken up directly, and that Night bury'd: Turn'd the Boatfwain out of our Tent for breeding Quarrels; his turbulent Temper was fo well known to the Captain, that he exprefs'd himfelf pleas'd at our turning him out, and faid he was furpriz'd we ever admitted him among us.

On the 17th, the Carpenter at Work on the Long Boat: The Surgeon's Mate this Day took out of Mr. *Cozens*'s Cheek a Ball much flatted, and a Piece of Bone, fuppofed to be Part of the Upper Jaw, which was defired by Mr. *Cozens* to be deliver'd to me; I receiv'd it, with the firft Ball mention'd to have been loft.

Thurfday the 18th, the Carpenter cut the Long-Boat in two, and lengthen'd her eleven Feet ten Inches and half by the Keel.

Sunday the 21ft, went aboard the Ship; but it being dangerous going about any

Thing,

Thing, .by Reafon of her working much, and a great Sea tumbling in, the Boats were employ'd in going about the Rocks in Search of Subfiftence.

The 22d, the Carpenter went with the Boat up the Bay to feek the *Indians*, but faw nothing of them; at Night the Boat return'd, the People having fhot Abundance of wild Fowl.

The 23d, the Lieutenant went with the Boat, and found the *Indians* juft come from the Place where they catch Seal; their Canoes were loaded with Seal, Sheep, and Oil.

Wednefday the 24th, departed this Life Mr. *Henry Cozens*, Midfhipman, after languifhing fourteen Days with the Wound he had receiv'd in his Cheek: We bury'd him in as decent a Manner as Time, Place, and Circumftances would allow. There have died fundry Ways fince the Ship firft ftruck forty-five Men; feven have deferted from us, and ftill continue away; remain and now victual'd one hundred Men.

Thurfday the 25th, the Wind at W. N. W. and rainy Weather; faw the *Indians* coming towards us in their Canoes; but the Deferters fettling where they took their Habitation when firft we faw 'em, by their rowing, we
thought

thought they were defign'd to go there; and
knowing the Deferters intended to take one
of their Canoes to go over to the Main, we
therefore launch'd the Yawl and went off to
them; there were five Canoes of 'em, laden
with Seal, Shell-fifh, and four Sheep; they
brought with 'em their Wives and Children,
fo that in all they were about fifty in Num‐
ber; they hawl'd their Canoes up, and built
four Wigg whams, which they cover'd with
the Bark of Trees and Seal-skins; we ima‐
gin'd by this they had an Intention to fettle
with us; they are a very fimple and inoffen‐
five People, of a low Stature, flat-nos'd, with
their Eyes funk very deep in their Heads;
they live continually in Smoak, and are never
without a Fire, even in their Canoes; they
have nothing to cover their Nakednefs, but
a Piece of an old Blanket, which they throw
over their Shoulders: We always fee 'em in
this Manner, notwithftanding we cloath 'em
whenever they come to us. By the Croffes
fet up in many Parts of the Land, one would
think they had fome Notion of the *Romifh*
Religion: We can't make 'em underftand us
by any Speech, nor by our Signs; we fhow'd
'em a Looking-glafs; when they faw the Re‐
prefentation of themfelves, they feem'd a-
maz'd,

maz'd, and fhow'd a thoufand antick Gef-
tures; and when once they beheld themfelves
in the Looking-glafs, they could hardly be
prevail'd on to look off.

On *Sunday* the 28th, in the Afternoon,
about twelve of the *Indian* Women went off in
their Canoes: We thought they were gone to
get Mufcles, but foon faw 'em diving; which
we imagin'd was for Pieces of Beef or Pork
that came out of the Wreck; but, when they
came afhore, we found they had been only
diving for Sea-Eggs. The Women among
thofe People feem to take more Pains for the
Provifions of Life than the Men; the latter
having little to do but to provide Wood, and
indulge themfelves by the Fire, while the
Women go every Tide a fifhing. To-day
we kill'd two *Indian* Sheep.

Monday the 29th, launch'd the Yawl to go
with the *Indians* to fhew us where they get
the Mufcles; but being too late for the Tide,
we came away without any: The Captain
fent to our Tent two Quarters of Mutton;
the Carpenter daily at work on the Long-
Boat. Winds variable.

On the 30th, the *Indian* Women went
again for Sea-Eggs, and brought a great
Quantity, with Abundance of white Mag-
gots

gots about three Quarters of an Inch in
Length, and in Circumference the Bignefs of
a Wheat-ftraw. Thefe Women keep an incredible Time under Water, with a fmall
Basket in their Hands, about the Size of the
Womens Work-baskets in *England*, into
which they put whatever they get in their
diving. Among thefe People the Order of
Nature feems inverted; the Males are ex-
empted from Hardfhips and Labour, and the
Women are meer Slaves and Drudges. This
Day one of our Seamen died: We obferve,
the *Indians* are very watchful of the Dead,
fitting continually near the above-mention'd
Corpfe, and carefully covering him; every
Moment looking on the Face of the Deceas'd
with Abundance of Gravity: At the Burial
their Deportment was grave and folemn;
feeing the People with their Hats off during
the Service, they were very attentive and
obfervant, and continued fo till the Burial
was over: They have nothing, as I have faid
before, but a Blanket to cover 'em, and the
Boys and Girls are quite naked, notwithftanding we felt it as cold here, as in the
hardeft Frofts in *England*, and almoft always
rainy.

Wednefday,

Wednesday, July the 1ft, employ'd in cutting Timbers in the Woods for the Long-Boat; rainy Weather; the Wind at S. W. the *Indian* Women diving for Food as before.

Thursday the 2d, laft Night the Store-Tent was broke open, and robbed of a great deal of Flower.

Monday the 6th, hard Gales of Wind, with Showers of Rain and Hail; came afhore from the Ship one Cask of Beef, with feveral of the Lower Deck Carlings, and Plank of the Upper and Lower Deck Beams; and, what was reckon'd very odd, the Cabbin-Bell came afhore, without its being faften'd to any Wood, or any one Thing of the Ship near it.

Tuefday the 7th, hard Gales of Wind, with Hail, Rain, and Lightning: The *Indian* Women went out as ufual in their Canoes to dive for Sea-Eggs, and brought afhore Abundance of 'em; they jump over-board out of their Canoe about a Mile from Shore; they take the Handle of their Baskets, which I have already defcribed, between their Teeth, and dive in five or fix Fathom Water; their Agility in Diving, and their Continuance under Water, for fo long a Time as they

generally

generally do, will be thought impoffible by
Perfons who have not been Eye-witneffes of
it; they feem as amphibious to us as Seals
and Allegators, and rarely make ufe of any
Provifion but what they get out of the Sea.

Wednefday the 8th, launch'd the Yawl and
went on Board; faw feveral Casks, fome of
Meat, and fome of Liquor; the Decks and
Sides abaft drove out, and entirely gone; the
Larboard Side abaft drove on Shore; about
two Miles and a half from the Tent a Cask
of Liquor was found, and broach'd by the
Perfon who found it, which was allow'd to
be a great Fault; he likewife broach'd a
Cask of Meat, which fhould have been preferv'd to carry away with us.

On *Thurfday* the 9th, the *Indians* with their
Wives and Children launch'd their Canoes,
and went away; 'tis believ'd they wanted
Provifions, fuch as Seal; they are indeed
never fettled long in a Place; it was faid
fome of our People wanted to have to do
with their Wives, which was the Reafon of
their going away fo foon. To-day we faw
feveral Things drive out of the Ship up the
Lagoon, as the Stump of the Main-Maft,
one of the Pumps, with one of the Gun-Car-
riages. Wind at N. W.

G

Friday the 10th, went aboard the Ship, found her broke afunder juſt at the Gangway ; faw the Cables out to the Windward, but could not fee any Casks of Liquor or Proviſions; went to ſhorter Allowance of Flower, one Pound for three Men *per Diem.* Laſt Night the Tent was robbed of half a Barrel of Flower : Orders were given by the Captain to watch the Store-Tent by Night ; all the Officers, the Marine included, with the Mates and Midſhipmen, were oblig'd to watch, the Captain and Carpenter alone excus'd, the Carpenter being every Day at work on the Long-Boat.

Friday the 17th, for this Week paſt hard Gales of Wind, with Rain and Hail as uſual. Laſt *Wedneſday* the Ship parted her Upper Works from the Lower Deck : Launch'd the Boat and went off to the Wreck, but could do nothing ; went up the Bay ; took a Quarter Cask, about three Parts full of Wine ; faw the *Indian* Dogs aſhore, but no People.

Saturday the 18th, launched the Boat, ſent her to the Wreck, and brought aſhore one Cask of Beef; it is believed ſome Guns were heard from the Sea : The Watch reported they have heard them two Nights paſt. Great

Diſtur-

Difturbances among the People. Wind at E.
N. E. and frofty Weather.

Sunday the 19th, launch'd the Boat, fent
her to the Wreck, hook'd a Cask fuppofed to
be Beef; but when towed afhore, we found
it contained nothing but Hatchets; we took
up along Shore, Abundance of Checque Shirts
in Dozens, alfo Caps, Bales of Cloth, and
Pieces of Beef and Pork.

Wednefday the 22d. This Day began to
build a Houfe to dwell in, finding our Stay
here, will be much longer than we at firft
expected.

The 23d, took up along Shore feveral
Pieces of Beef and Pork, Shirts, Caps, Frocks,
Trowfers, Pieces of Cloth, with other fer-
viceable Things, and Wax Candles of all
Sizes.

Saturday the 25th, hard Showers of Rain
and Hail; the Wind at North. Shot feveral
Sea-Gulls, Geefe, Hawks, and other Birds:
The Carpenter had this Day given him by
one of the People, a fine large Rock Crab,
it being the firft of the Kind we ever faw
here.

Sunday the 26th, moderate Gales and variable Winds, with Rain and Hail: Moft
Part of our People eat a Weed that grows on

the

the Rocks; it is a thin Weed of a dark green
Colour, and called by the Seamen, *Slaugh*. It
is furprifing how the black Currant Trees,
which are here in great Plenty, have budded
within thefe three Days. Began thatching
our new Houfe with Bufhes: To-day we
caught a fine Rock-Fifh; this is the firft Fifh
we have feen alive fince our being here. Obferving our new Town, we find there are no
lefs than eighteen Houfes in it.

Monday the 27th, launched the Boat, went
to the Wreck, but found nothing; clofe Weather, the Wind ftill at North: Rife the Sheers
for erecting a Tent over the Long-Boat to
keep the Men from being expofed to the continual Rains. This Day we finifhed the
Thatching of our new Houfe.

Wednefday the 29th, Frefh Gales at N. W.
with Rain; fure no Men ever met with fuch
Weather as we have in this Climate: To-day
we walked in the Woods to take fome notice
of the Trees, which we find to be very much
like our Beech in *England*; but the Trees
and Bufhes are in general of a foft free Nature, and with a fpicey Bark.

Thurfday the 30th, Wind ftill at N. W.
and rainy Weather. This Day departed this
Life *Nathaniel Robinfon*, the laft private Man
of

of the Invalids; there are now only two left,
viz. the Captain and Surgeon. Being at the
Honourable Mr. *B——n*'s Tent, I found him
looking in Sir *John Narborough*'s Voyage to
thefe Seas; this Book I defired the Loan of,
he told me it was Captain *C———p*'s, and
did not doubt but he would lend it me; this
Favour I requefted of the Captain, and it
was prefently granted. Carefully perufing
this Book, I conceived an Opinion that our
going through the *Streights of Magellan* for
the Coaft of *Brafil*, would be the only Way
to prevent our throwing ourfelves into the
Hands of a cruel, barbarous, and infulting
Enemy: Our Long-Boat, when finifhed, can
be fit for no Enterprize, but the Prefervation
of Life: As we cannot act offenfively, we
ought to have Regard to our Safety and Liberty. This Evening Propofals were offered
to the Officers concerning our going through
the *Streights of Magellan*; which at this Time
they feem to approve of.

Friday the 31ft, hard Gales at N. W.
with Rain: This Day was taken up along
Shore an Otter juft killed, but by what Animal we could not tell; it was bleeding frefh
when taken up, and proved a dainty Repaft.

paft. Came afhore the Ship's Beams, with feveral Things of great Value.

Saturday, Auguft the 1ft, hard Gales at N. W. with Rain and Hail. This Day put to an Allowance of Flower, one Quarter of a Pound a Man *per Diem*, and one Pint of Wine; thofe who like Brandy, to have half a Pint in Lieu of Wine. We have now in a manner nothing to live on but what we pick up along the Shore: The Ship's Company agree to go through the *Streights of Magellan*.

Sunday the 2d, This Morning found the Store Tent robbed of Brandy; filled up all the ullage Casks; picked up about the Rocks Abundance of Clams, a Shell-fifh not unlike our Cockles: Thefe Fifh are at prefent the Support of our Life. The People are now very quarrelfome and difcontented.

Monday the 3d, this Day having fine Weather, (which is a Prodigy in this Place) launched the Boat, and went about the Rocks and Iflands on Difcovery. This Day we alfo moved into our new Houfe, it being a very commodious Habitation, exceedingly well thatched; in this Dwelling there are Cabbins for fourteen People, which are covered infide and out with broad Cloath: This is a rich Houfe, and, in fome Parts of the World, would

would purchafe a pretty Eftate; there are feveral hundred Yards of Cloth about it, befides
the Curtains and Linings, which are Shalloon
and Camblet; in fhort, confidering where
we are, we cannot defire a better Habitation.
The People fall into Difputes concerning the
Boat, where we are to proceed with her,
when fhe is built and ready for going off. It
is the Opinion of the Navigators, that going
through the *Streights of Magellan* is the fafeft
and only Way to preferve Life and Liberty:
The Artifts, who have worked the Bearings
and Diftance, are very preffing that it fhould
be moved to the Captain, purpofing to
have their Reafons drawn up, and figned by
all who are willing to go that Way, and to
be delivered to the Captain for his Opinion;
upon this there was a Paper drawn up, and
as foon as the People heard it, they came
flocking to fign firft, crying all aloud for the
Streights, feeming overjoyed, as if they were
going to *England* directly, without any Affliction or Trouble; but there muft be a great
deal of Hardfhip to be encountered before we
arrive at our native Country: This Paper
was figned by all the Officers on the Spot,
except the Captain, Lieutenant, Purfer, and
Surgeon, and by all the Seamen in general,
except the Captain's Steward.

Tuefday

Tuefday the 4th, at the Time of ferving at the Store-houfe, about Twelve o'Clock, I went to the Captain, with the Mafter, Carpenter, and Boatfwain, and read to him the Paper; he anfwered, he would confider of it, and give his Anfwer : Here follows a Copy of the Paper figned.

WE whofe Names are under-mentioned, do, upon mature Confideration, as we have met with fo happy a Deliverance, think it the beft, fureft, and moft fafe Way, for the Prefervation of the Body of People on the Spot, to proceed through the *Streights of Magellan* for *England*. Dated at a defolate Ifland on the Coaft of *Patagonia*, in the Latitude of 47 Deg. 00 Min. South, and Weft Longitude from the Meridian of *London* 81 Deg. 40 Min. in the *South-Seas*, this 2d Day of *Auguft* 1741.

John Bulkeley, Gunner
John Cummins, Carpenter
Thomas Clark, Mafter
John King, Boatfwain
John Jones, Mafter's Mate
John Snow, ditto
Robert Elliot, Surgeon s Mate
The Hon. *John Byron*, Midfhipman
Alexander Campbell, ditto
Ifaac Morris, ditto
Thomas Maclean, Cook

John

John Mooring, Boatſwain's Mate
Richard Phipps, ditto
John Young, Cooper
Richard Noble, Quarter-Maſter
William Roſe, ditto
William Hervey, Quarter-Gunner
John Boſman, Seaman
William Moore, ditto
Samuel Stook, ditto
Samuel Cooper, ditto
David Buckley, Quarter-Gunner
Henry Stevens
Benjamin Smith
John Montgomery
John Duck
John Hayes
James Butler
John Hart
James Roach
Job Barns
John Petman
William Callicutt
George Smith
Peter Deleroy
James Mac Cawle
John George
John Shorclan
Richard Eaſt
William Lane
William Oram
Moſes Lewis
Nicholas Griſelham

Seamen.

H   We

We whofe Names are under-mention'd, have had fufficient Reafons, from the abovemention'd People, to confent to go this Way. Sign'd by

Capt. *Robert Pemberton*, Commander of his Majefty's Land-Forces.

William Fielding, } Lieutenants.
Robert Ewers,

Wednefday the 5th, this Day I went with the Mafter, Carpenter, Mafter's Mates, and Midfhipmen, to the Captain, to acquaint him with what was done, and refolv'd on; and farther told him, It was a Duty incumbent on us to preferve Life before any other Intereft. He anfwer'd, Gentlemen, I defire Time to confider of it, and will give you my final Determination; on which we took our Leave, and came away.

Thurfday the 6th, hard Gales at W.S.W. and rainy Weather. At Noon went with Mr. *Cummins* to Captain *P—mb—rt—n's* Tent, to have fome farther Conference for our future Deliverance: While we were there, the Captain fent his Service to Captain *C—p* for a Pair of Pocket-Piftols, his own Property, which had been refufed him on his Requeft fome Time before. The Servant

was

was anfwer'd, by the Captain's Favourite and Prime Minifter the Steward, The Captain is ill, and I can't let you have 'em. This Anfwer not being fatisfactory to Capt. *P—mb—rt—n,* he fent a fecond Time, and infifted on the Delivery of his Piftols; but was anfwer'd, they could not be come at before the Captain was up; but a little Time after it was judg'd proper to fend Captain *P—mb—rt—n* his Piftols. From Captain *P—mb—rt—n*'s we went to the L——t's Tent; while there, the L——t was fent for to Captain *C——p*; about an Hour after the Carpenter and my-felf were fent for; when we came to him, he faid, Gentlemen, I have maturely confi-der'd the Contents of your Paper, fo far as it regards the Prefervation of the People on the Spot: This Paper has given me a great deal of Uneafinefs, infomuch that I have not clos'd my Eyes till Eight o'Clock this Morn-ing, for thinking of it; but, I think, you have not weigh'd the Thing rightly; do you know we are above one hundred and fixty Leagues diftant S. W. from the *Streights of Ma-gellan,* with the Wind againft us? Then think on the Diftance to be run afterwards on the other Side the *Streights,* with the Wind always againft us, and where no Water is to be

had. I anfwer'd, Sir, you fay it is above one
hundred and fixty Leagues to the *Streights*;
but let the Navigators work it, and they will
find it not above ninety Leagues; yourfelf
and Lieutenant are undoubtedly Navigators
and Judges, therefore will certainly find it as
I fay. Mr. *Cummins* acquainted him, according to his Calculation, the Veffel would
carry a Month's Water, at a Quart a Man
per Diem; and, Sir, do you confider, after
running a-long Shore to the Northward this
Side the Land, that we have one hundred
Leagues to run right out to Sea to the Ifland of
Juan Ferdinandez; and five hundred Chances
to one, if we meet the Commodore there,
or any of the Squadron; nor do we know
but the Commodore may have fhared the
fame Fate with ourfelves, or perhaps worfe?
The Captain anfwer'd, It's a thoufand to one
if we fee the Commodore at *Juan Ferdinandez*; for, Gentlemen, to let you into a
Secret, which I never difcover'd before, we
fhall meet him at *Baldavia*, his Orders were
from ―――― to go there with the Squadron,
it being a Place of little or no Force. Mr.
Cummins anfwer'd, Sir, 'tis agreed, the Commodore is at *Baldavia*; but we make it in our
Bargain, when we go from hence, that we
will

will put afhore at every Place when we want Water, whenever the Weather will permit, without any Obftruction. The Captain reply'd, There is no Occafion for that; we will water at the Iflands, and take a Veffel going along. Mr. *Cummins* faid, Sir, what fhall we do with a Veffel, without Provifions, for ninety Souls? The Captain anfwer'd, We will take a Veffel loaden with Flower from *Chili*, there being a great many Trading Veffels that Way; and then we will proceed through the *Streights of Magellan.* Mr. *Cummins* faid, How fhall we take a Veffel without Guns? not having any but Muskets; and our Enemies know, as well as ourfelves, that we have a Squadron in thefe Seas, therefore undoubtedly are well arm'd, and keep a good Look-out. The Captain's Anfwer to this was, What are our fmall Arms for, but to board 'em? The Carpenter faid, Sir, if a Shot fhould take the Boat under Water it would not be in my Power to ftop a Leak of that kind, where the Plank is fo thin, that in fome Places it is not above three Quarters of an Inch thick. The Captain then faid, Gentlemen, I am agreeable to any Thing, and willing to go any Way, for the Prefervation of the People; but at the fame Time would

would have you confider of it, the Wind being always againſt us on the other Side the
Land, and we have above ſeven hundred
Leagues to the River *Plate*.   I anſwer'd the
Captain,'Tis not above five hundred and ninety Leagues from hence to Cape St. *Antonio*'s ;
and, as I have before ſaid, let the Navigators
work it, and Reaſon take Place, which is
what we chiefly deſire to be govern'd by :
Another Inducement we have to go the Way
propos'd is, that we may be aſſur'd of Water
and Proviſion.   I allow that, ſays the Captain, and we may ſave our own ; but how
do you know whether we may not meet
Enemies in the *Streights?*   I reply'd to the
Captain, We can have no Enemies to encounter there, but *Indians* in their Canoes,
and thoſe we can maſter at our Pleaſure.
The Captain then ſeem'd to countenance our
Opinion again ; and ſaid, When we come to
St. *Julian*'s we ſhall be ſure of Salt in Plenty
for our Proviſions, without which our Fowls
will not keep above two or three Days :
Beſides, when we come to the River *Plate*,
we may meet with a Prize, they not being
acquainted with any *Engliſh* Veſſel like ours,
with Schooner's Sails ; by which Means we
may run up the River, and take a larger
Veſſel :

Veſſel : If we fail here, we may go aſhore,
and get what Cattle we pleaſe; but what
Buſineſs have we at the *Rio Grand?* We
muſt go to the *Rio Janeiro.* I told him, we
ſhould be oblig'd to ſtop at every Place a-long
Shore for Supplies; at St. *Catharine*'s the Governor will give us a Certificate, ſo that we
ſhall be known to be the People that were
there in the Squadron. The Captain ſaid,
That's true, and I can get Bills of Credit in
any Part of *Brazil*; beſides, the People may
be ſeparated, ſome in the *Flota*, and ſome in
other Ships; with leſs Hands we may go to
Barbadoes. Mr. *Cummins* told him, We might
venture to *England* with twelve Hands. Yes,
you may, ſays the Captain, with thirty. It
is to be obſerv'd, during all this Debate, the
Lieutenant ſpoke not a Word. The Carpenter asking him the Reaſon of his Silence in
all the Conſultation, he anſwer'd, I'll give my
Opinion hereafter. The Captain ſaid, I knew
nothing of his being acquainted with it, till
Mr. *Bulkeley* told me Yeſterday; but at the
ſame Time, Mr. *B——s*, I expect you will
be the firſt that will ſign the Paper. I imagin'd the Captain meant our Paper, and immediately anſwer'd, with ſome Warmth, As
he had refus'd ſigning at firſt, and at the
ſame

fame Time agreed to the Propofal, that I had fign'd fo clofe, that there was no Room left for his Name, and now it was too late for him to fign. The Captain furpriz'd me, by faying, I don't mean your Paper. I told him, Any other, which fhould be contrary to ours, would never be fign'd by us. Mr. *Cummins* faid to the Captain, Sir, 'tis all owing to you that we are here; if you had confulted your Officers, we might have avoided this Misfortune; confidering the Condition the Ship was in, fhe was not fit to come in with the Land, all our Men being fick, and not above three Seamen in a Watch; fuppofe the Maft had gone by the Board, as was every Moment expected. The Captain made Anfwer, Gentlemen, you do not know my Orders, there never were any fo ftrict given to a Commander before; and had I but two Men living befides myfelf, I muft, and was obliged to go to the firft Rendezvous, which was the Ifland of *Noftra Senbora di Socora:* I was obliged to go there at all Events. I made Anfwer to this, Sir, if that is the Cafe, it feems plain, the Thing was defign'd we fhould be here: But, Sir, I am of Opinion, notwithftanding the Commodore had his Orders from ——— to go with the Squadron to *Baldavia*,

that

that at the fame Time thofe Orders were fo
far difcretional, that if the Squadron was dif-
abled, Care was to be taken not to endanger
his Majefty's Ships.   Yes, that (fays the Captain) was fettled at St. *Julian*'s : Notwithftanding what has been faid, Gentlemen, I
am agreeable to take any Chance with you,
and to go any Way; but would have you
confider of it, and defer your Determination
till all is ready to go off the Spot.   I then
told the Captain, You have known, Sir, from
the Time you faw the Propofal, that the
People are uneafy, and the Work is at a
Stand, and in this Situation Things will be
until this Affair is fettled ; therefore the fooner
you refolve, the better.   The Captain reply'd, I defign to have a Confultation among
my Officers : Have you any more Objections
to make ?   I anfwer'd, Yes, Sir, one more;
which is, when you go from hence, you are
not to weigh, come to an Anchor, or alter
Courfe, without confulting your Officers.
The Captain faid, Gentlemen, I was your
Commander till the Ship parted, or as long
as any Stores or Provifions were getting out
of her.   We told him, we had always taken
Care to obey his Orders in the ftricteft Manner; which he allow'd us to have done; and

I   he

he added, You were the Officers that I placed
my whole Dependence in. We anſwer'd,
Sir, we will ſupport you with our Lives, as
long as you ſuffer Reaſon to rule; and then
we parted. After this Conſultation the Captain ſeldom came out of his Tent, which occaſion'd great Diſturbances among the People.

Friday the 7th, the Wind at W. N. W.
with Rain. This Day the Navigators work'd
the Bearings and Diſtance along Shore, from
one Place to another, to know the true Diſtance: Hereupon it was agreed to proceed
through the *Streights of Magellan*, according
to Sir *John Narborough*'s Directions, which
give us great Encouragement to go that Way.
Captain *P————n* draw'd his Men up, and
diſmiſs'd 'em again. Great Uneaſineſs among
the People.

Saturday the 8th, this Morning went to
the Lieutenant, for him to acquaint the Captain all his Officers were ready to give ſufficient Reaſons for going through the *Streights
of Magellan*, deſiring a Conſultation might
be held in the Afternoon. At Three o'Clock
the Captain ſent for me and Mr. *Cummins*;
when we came, the Maſter and Boatſwain
were ſent for, but they were gone in Search
of Subſiſtence, as Limpetts, Muſcles, *&c.*
                                    The

The Captain faid, Gentlemen, I don't doubt
but you have confider'd upon the Bufinefs you
are come about; therefore I am determin'd
to take my Fate with you, or where the
Spirit of the People leads, and fhall ufe my
beft Endeavours for their Prefervation; but
I am afraid of meeting contrary Winds, for
after the Sun has crofs'd the Line we muft
expect to meet 'em. I made Anfwer, By all
Accounts, the Wind hangs from N. W. to
the S. W. above three Parts of the Year;
which is in our Favour. Mr. *Cummins* told
him, There was frefh Water to be got as
well on one Coaft as the other; and if
Sir *John Narborough*'s Treatment was fo ill
in a profound Peace, what muft we expect
in a Time of open War? The Captain faid,
I am afraid, very bad. Then Mr. *Cummins*
fpoke in this Manner to the Captain: Sir, I
always took you for an honourable Gentleman, and I believe you to be fuch; on
your Honour, Sir, I beg you will give the
true Sentiments of your Mind, whether thro'
the *Streights* is not the fureft and fafeft Way
to preferve our Lives, notwithftanding we
have a thoufand Difficulties to encounter
with any way? The Captain anfwer'd, I
really think going to the Northward is the

fafeft

safeft Way; for fuppofe we fhould be drove off to Sea, when on the other Side the Land, what is to be done then? I faid, Sir, it is our Bufinefs to keep the Shore, to prevent all Accidents that may happen that way. Then Lieutenant *B — s* made an Objection, Suppofe you have the Wind blowing right in, and a tumbling Sea, as to endanger the Boat, what are we to do? I made Anfwer, Sir, if you remember, when we were riding at St. *Ju-lian*'s, it blow'd a very hard Gale of Wind right in from the Sea; yet, even then, the Sea did not run fo high as to endanger a Boat riding at Anchor: Another Inftance I bring you from St. *Catharine*'s, when we had fuch hard Gales, that the *Tryal* loft her Mafts, and the *Pearl* feparated from the Squadron; yet, at that Time, there was no Sea compa-rable to what we have met with this Side the Land. The Lieutenant allow'd this to be Fact. Then the Captain faid, I will allow you to have Water at *Port Defire*; but do you confider the lengthening your Diftance, by keeping along Shore, and rounding every Bay, and fome of thofe Bays are very deep. I told him, That undoubtedly there was Wa-ter all along the Coaft, and that we had no Bufinefs to round the Bays, but to fteer from

one

one Head-land to the other. Then Lieutenant *B*—*s* made a fecond Objection, Suppofe we are forced into a Bay, and Shoalwater? I anfwer'd, We fhould always have
a Boat a-head, and our Draught of Water
will not be above four or five Feet at moft;
and if we fhould be fo unfortunate as to lofe
our Boat, we muft keep the Lead a going.
The L——t reply'd, That was true, and
there could not be a great deal of Difficulty
in it. This was the only Time the L——t
ever fpoke in Publick on the Affair; he
always allow'd, when abfent from the Captain, that going through the *Streights* was
the beft Way; but in the Captain's Prefence
he fided with him, and was for going to the
Northward.

Sunday the 9th, at Three this Afternoon,
I went with Mr. *Cummins*, the Mafter, and
Boatfwain, as defir'd, to the Captain, to give
him our Opinions, believing, going thro' the
Streights the fureft Way to preferve Life: It
was therefore agreed, That if the Wind did
not fet in againft us, at the Sun's croffing
the Line, that the Captain would go that
Way. The Captain ask'd every Man's Opinion, and found the People unanimous for
the *Streights of Magellan.* To-day, being
fair

fair Weather, launch'd the Yawl to go a fowling; fhot feveral Geefe, Ducks, Shaggs, and Sea-pies. Heel'd the Long-Boat for planking.

Monday the 10th, Wind at N. and N.N.W. Rainy Weather. Eat Slaugh and Sea-weed fry'd with Tallow-Candles, which we pick'd up along Shore; this we reckon at prefent exceeding good Eating, having nothing to live on but a Quarter of a Pound of Flower a Man *per* Day, and what we can get off the Rocks; for many Days the Weather has been fo bad, that we have not been able to ftir abroad, tho' almoft ftarv'd for want of Food.

Tuefday the 11th, hard Gales at S.W. with heavy Rains. This Afternoon the People came in Arms to acquaint us of the Stores being robbed; they therefore wanted our Confent for moving the Stores to our Tent; on which we defir'd they would defift from offering any Violence; we told 'em of the ill Confequence of Mutiny, which, as we always abhor'd, we took all imaginable Care to prevent: The People, on our Perfuafions, inftantly quitted their Arms. The Captain prefently fent for me and Mr. *Cummins,* to acquaint us with what had happen'd: He

told

told us the Purfer, accidentally coming by, faw the Prifoner *Rowland Cruffett*, Marine, crawling from the Bufhes, and from under the Store-Tent, and found on him upwards of a Day's Flower for ninety Souls, with one Piece of Beef under his Coat, and three Pieces more, which were conceal'd in the Bufhes, to carry off when an Opportunity offer'd; and the Centry, *Thomas Smith*, his Mefs-mate, a Marine, undoubtedly was privy to the Robbery. The Captain farther faid, We have nothing to do with them; but I fhall fend to Captain *P——n*, to infift on a Court-Martial: I really think, that for robbing the Store-Tent, (which, in our prefent Circumftances, is ftarving the whole Body. of People) the Prifoners deferve Death. This was not only the Captain's Opinion, but indeed the Sentiments of every Perfon prefent. After we parted from the Captain, we were fent for by Capt. *P——n:* He acquainted us, he would go as far as the Martial Law would allow him, and in Conjunction with the Sea-Officers: I look (faid he) on the L——t as nothing, and the C——n in the fame Light: As for you two, (meaning the Gunner and Carpenter) I confide in, and fhall have Regard to your Opinions. When the Articles
of

of War were read, we found their Crime did
not touch Life, but that they were to fuffer
Corporal Punifhment. Whilft Mr. *Cummins*
was laying open the Nature of their Guilt,
and the ill Confequence of Lenity in the Circumftances we were in, I propos'd a Way,
next to Death; which was, if judg'd proper
by Captain *P——n* and Captain *C——p,* to
carry 'em off to an Ifland where the Ship
parted, there being Mufcles, Limpetts, and
Clams in Abundance, and no want of Water,
and there to be left till we fhould be ready
for failing; and, to ftrike a Terror in all for
the future, that if any Man fhould be guilty
of the like Offence, without any Refpect of
Perfon, he fhould fhare the fame Fate. This
Propofal was approved of by both the Cap-
tains. At Night Lieutenant *B——n* furpriz'd
us with a new kind of Propofal we little
dreamt of, which was, to have a proper
Place of Devotion, to perform Divine Service in every Sabbath-Day: For this Sacred
Office our Tent was judg'd the moft commodious Place. The Duty of Publick Prayer
had been entirely neglected on Board, tho'
every Seaman pays Four-pence *per* Month
towards the Support of a Minifter; yet Devotion, in fo folemn a Manner, is fo rarely
perform'd,

perform'd, that I know but one Inftance of it during the many Years I have belong'd to the Navy. We believe Religion to have the leaft Share in this Propofal of the Lieute-nant. If our Tent fhould be turn'd into a Houfe of Prayer, and this Project takes, we may, perhaps, in the Midft of our Devotion, be furpriz'd, and our Arms taken from us, in order to fruftrate our Defigns, and pre-vent our Return to *England* through the *Streights of Magellan*, or any other Way.

Wednefday the 12th, hard Gales from S. W. to W. with heavy Showers of Hail and Rain. Serv'd out Provifions To-day, a Piece of Beef for four Men ; fome Time paft we have had but a Quarter of a Pound of Flower *per* Man *per Diem*, and three Pieces of Beef; we live chiefly on Mufcles, Limpitts, and Clams, with Saragraza and Thromba ; one is a green broad Weed, common on the Rocks in *England*; the other is a round Sea-weed, fo large, that a Man ean fcarce grafp it ; it grows in the Sea, with broad Leaves ; this laft we boil, the Saragraza we fry in Tallow ; in this Manner we fupport Life : Even thefe Shell-fifh and Weeds we get with great Difficulty ; for the Wind, the Rain, and Coldnefs of the Cli-mate in this Seafon, are fo extremely fevere,

K   that

that a Man will paufe fome Time whether
he fhall ftay in his Tent and ftarve, or go
out in Queft of Food.

Friday the 14th, very hard Gales at W.
and N. W. with Showers of Rain and Hail,
which beat with fuch Violence againft a
Man's Face, that he can hardly withftand it ;
however, one of our Mefs-mates To-day
fhot three Gulls and a Hawk; which gave
us a very elegant Repaft. This Day was
held a Court-Martial on the Centry who is
believ'd Confederate with the Marine that
robbed the Store-Tent: Sentence was pafs'd
on 'em to receive fix hundred Lafhes each:
Captain *C——p*, not thinking the Punifhment adequate to the Crime, cut 'em fhort
of their Allowance; fo that they have now
but half the Provifions they had before: The
Day following the Offenders receiv'd two
hundred Lafhes each, as Part of their Punifhment. We hawl'd the Long-Boat higher up,
for fear the Sea fhould wafh the Blocks from
under her. We have found out a new Way
of managing the Slaugh; we fry it in thin
Batter with Tallow, and ufe it as Bread.

Sunday the 16th, Frefh Gales of Wind at
S. W. with heavy Showers of Hail: The
People generally complain of a Malady in
their

their Eyes; they are in great Pain, and can scarce see to walk about. The last Tide flowed nine Feet perpendicular; To-day we picked up Shell-Fish in Abundance, with Pieces of Beef and Pork. The Prisoners received two hundred Lashes more.

Tuesday the 18th, this Day the Carpenter, who has all along been indefatigable in working about the Long-Boat, saw one of the Seamen cutting up an Anchor-Stock for Fire-Wood, which had been designed for a particular Use for the Boat; at Sight of the Fellow's Folly he could not contain himself: This Affair, added to the little Concern and intolerable Indifference that appeared in the Generality of the People, for some Time impaired his Understanding, and made him delirious; all possible Methods are used to restore him, as he is the only Man, who, through the Assistance of Providence, can compleat the Means of our Deliverance.

Wednesday the 19th, The Carpenter was so much recovered, that he went to Work as usual; at Night, the Lieutenant acquainted us, that the Captain desired to speak with the Carpenter and me To-morrow at Noon, to consult what should be done with the two Prisoners, having received but four hundred

Lafhes out of the fix, to which they were
fentenced by a Court-Martial, the other two
hundred being remitted by their own Officers.

Thurfday the 20th, We waited on the
Captain, who acquainted us with what the
Lieutenant had mentioned laft Night relating
to the Prifoners: We told him the People
were very uneafy about this Mitigation of
the Punifhment inflicted on them by a Court
Martial; therefore it was agreed they fhould
provide for themfelves as well as they could;
but to have no Sort of Provifions out of the
Store-Tent for the future.

Saturday the 22d, We begun upon feveral
Contrivances to get Provifions, fuch as building Punts, Cask-Boats, Leather-Boats, and
the like.

On *Sunday* the 23d, The Store-Tent was
again robbed, and, on Examination, was
found a Deficiency of twelve Days Brandy
for ninety Men: The Lieutenant, myfelf,
and Carpenter went to the Captain to confult
fome Way which might effectually prevent
thofe villainous Practices for the future; the
Captain defired us to make a nice Enquiry
into this Robbery, being determined to in-
flict the fevereft Punifhment on the Offenders;

ders; tho' it would give him the greateft
Concern if any innocent Perfon fhould fuffer.
This Day we confined one of the Centinels
for being drunk on his Poft; the Day following the Boatfwain gave us Information of the
Perfons who had robbed the Tent; they
were two Centinels, *Smith* and *Butler*;
thofe very Perfons were the firft who infifted,
that the Seamen, as well as themfelves, fhould
watch the Store-Tent; their own Officers, as
yet, have brought them to no Examination:
We have alfo Information that the Purfer
holds frequent Converfation with the Rebels,
contrary to all the Laws of the Navy, fupplying them with Liquors in Abundance, to
the great Diftrefs of his Majefty's faithful
Subjects, who have but half a Pint *per* Day
to fubfift on. There are now great Difturbances among the People concerning going
to the Northward; they believe Captain
C———p never intended to return to *England* by his propofing this Way, in Oppofition
to the Opinion of all the Navigators, who
have given Reafons for going thro' the*Streights
of Magellan.* There is a Sort of a Party-
Rage among the People, fomented by a kind
of Bribery that has more Influence on the
Seamen than Money; there are fome daily
bought

bought off by Rum, and other ſtrong Liquors. Unleſs a Stop is put to theſe Proceedings, we ſhall never go off the Spot.

Tueſday the 25th, This Day felt four great Earthquakes, three of which were very terrible; notwithſtanding the violent Shocks and Tremblings of the Earth, we find no Ground ſhifted. Hard Gales of Wind at North, with heavy Showers of Rain.

Thurſday the 27th, The Diſturbances increaſe among the People; we plainly ſee there is a Party raiſed to go to the Northward; we went to the Lieutenant, and conſulted with him what was to be done in the preſent Exigence; myſelf being reckoned the Projeƈtor of the Scheme for going through the *Streights* was threatened to be ſhot by *Noble* the Quarter-Maſter: After having ſome Diſcourſe with the Lieutenant, he told me, If I would draw up a Paper for the Captain to ſign, in order to ſatisfy the People, that he would go to the Southward, and every Officer to have a Copy of it, to juſtify himſelf in *England*, it would be as proper a Method as we could take. The Paper was immediately drawn up in theſe Words, *viz.*

W H E R E-

WHEREAS upon a General Consultation, it has been agreed to go
from this Place through the *Streights of Magellan*, for the Coaft of *Brazil*, in our Way
for *England:* We do, notwithftanding, find
the People feparating into Parties, which
muft confequently end in the Deftruction of
the whole Body; and as alfo there have been
great Robberies committed on the Stores,
and every Thing is now at a Stand; therefore, to prevent all future Frauds and Ani-
mofities, we are unanimoufly agreed to proceed as above-mention'd.

This Paper was deliver'd to the Lieutenant,
who faid that he was fure the Captain would
fign it; but in Cafe of Refufal, he fhould be
confin'd for fhooting Mr. *Cozens*, and he
would take the Command on himfelf: And,
to prevent further Difturbances, the Purfer,
as he much convers'd with the Rebels, it is
agreed, by the Body of Officers, to fend him
off the Ifland, for acting fo contrary to his
Duty, in Contempt of the Articles of War,
the Laws of his Country, and the known
Rules of the Navy. It was likewife agreed,
that any Perfon, who engaged himfelf in
raifing

raifing Parties, fhould be difarm'd. By this Day's Proceedings, 'we thought the Lieutenant a Gentleman of Refolution; but the Words and Actions of People do not always concur.

Friday the 28th, To-day the Officers and People all appear'd in Arms. The Mafter, Boatfwain, Gunner, and Carpenter, with Mr. *J*——*s* Mate, and Mr. *C*——*ll* Midfhipman, went into the Captain's Tent, the Lieutenant being with him. As foon as the Officers were feated, a Confultation was held concerning *Smith* and *Butler* robbing the Store-Tent; they were fentenced to be tranfported to the Main, or fome Ifland. As foon as this Affair was over, we talk'd to the Captain of the Uneafinefs among the People; that there had been a long Time a vifible Inquietude among 'em, and that we could not help feeing there were Schemes form'd to obftruct our Defign in going to the Southward. The Captain anfwer'd, Gentlemen, it is Time enough to think of this when we are ready to go off: Have not I told you before, that I do not care which Way I go, Southward or Northward? I will take my Fate with you. Every body now expected the Lieutenant to reply, efpecially after the Zeal he exprefs'd himfelf

himfelf with the Day before; but he fate
fpeechlefs, without any Regard to the Welfare of the People, or to his own Propofals.
Finding he did not move in the Affair, I took
out the Paper which was agreed to by the
Lieutenant and the reft of the Officers, and
read it to the Captain, and ask'd him to fign
it; which he ftrenuoufly oppos'd, and feem'd
very much enrag'd that it fhould be propos'd
to him. Upon this we dropt the Matter,
and began to difcourfe concerning the Provifions: We thought it neceffary, that ten
Weeks Subfiftence fhould be fecur'd to carry
with us, and that the Liquor fhould be buried
Under-ground; but he gave us no Anfwer.
Finding no Relief here, we went to Captain
P———*n*'s Tent, to confult with him what
we fhould do in the prefent Exigence. On
our coming out from the Captain, we faw a
Flag hoifted on Captain *P*——*n*'s Tent, the
Captain himfelf feated in a Chair, furrounded
by the People. On feeing this, all the Officers
prefent at the Confultation, except the Lieutenant, went over to Captain *P*——*n*. Here
it was agreed, in Cafe the Captain perfifted
to refufe figning the Paper, to take the Command from him, and to give it the Lieutenant,
according to the Lieutenant's own Propofal.

L   At

At the fame Time Captain *P——n* told the
People, he would ftand by 'em with his Life,
in going through the *Streights of Magellan,*
the Way propos'd in the Paper.   The People
gave three Cheers, crying aloud for *England.*
The Captain hearing the Noife, got out of
Bed to his Tent-Door, and call'd the People,
enquiring what they wanted; then fent for
all the Officers: He was then told, fince he
refus'd figning the Paper, and had no Regard
to the Safety of our Provifions, the People
unanimoufly agreed to take the Command
from him, and transfer it to the Lieutenant.
Hearing this, with an exalted Voice, Captain
C——p fays, Who is he that will take the
Command from me?   Addreffing himfelf to
the Lieutenant, Is it you, Sir?   The Lieutenant reply'd, No, Sir.   The Terror of the
Captain's Afpect intimidated the Lieutenant
to that Degree, that he look'd like a Ghoft.
We left him with the Captain, and return'd
to Captain *P——n*'s Tent, to acquaint him
of the Lieutenant's refufing the Command.
We had not been long here before Captain
C——p fent for us.   I was the firft Perfon
call'd for; at my entering his Tent, I faw
him feated on a Cheft, with a cock'd Piftol
on his Right Thigh; obferving this, I defir'd

Mr. *J*—*s*, who was the Mate he always re-
ly'd on for Navigation, to tell the Captain, I
did not think proper to come before a cock'd
Piftol: Notwithftanding I was arm'd, I drew
back, altho' I had my Piftol cock'd, and there
were feveral Men near me arm'd with Muf-
kets. The Captain's perfonal Bravery no
Man doubted of; his Courage was exceffive,
and made him rafh and defperate; his fhooting Mr. *Cozens* was a fatal Proof of it; he
was grown more defperate by this unhappy
Action, and was obferv'd fince feldom to be-
have himfelf with any Compofure of Mind.
It is a Piece of human Prudence to retreat
from a Man in a Phrenzy, becaufe he who
does not value his own Life, has another
Man's in his Power. I had no Defire of falling by the Hand of Captain *C*——*p*, and
fhould be greatly difturb'd to be compell'd,
for my own Prefervation, to difcharge a
Piftol at a Gentleman againft whom I never
had any Spleen, and who was my Commander. When Mr. *J*——*s* acquainted him with
what I defired him, the Captain threw his
Piftol afide, and came out of his Tent; he
told the People, he would go with them to
the Southward; he defired to know their
Grievances, and he would redrefs them: They

all

all call'd out for their Sea-Store of Provisions to be secur'd, and the rest equally divided. Here the Captain show'd all the Conduct and Courage imaginable; he was a single Man against a Multitude, all of 'em dissatisfy'd with him, and all of 'em in Arms : He told 'em the ill Consequence of sharing the Provisions, that it was living To-day and starving To-morrow; but the People were not to be satisfy'd, the Officers had now no Authority over 'em, and they were some Time deaf to their Persuasions; nay, it was with Difficulty that they could dissuade 'em from pulling down the Store-Tent, and taking away the Provisions by Force; they remov'd the Provisions out of the Store-Tent, then fell to digging a Hole to bury the Brandy ; the Sea-Store to be secur'd, the Remainder to be immediately shar'd. Had this been comply'd with, the Consequences might have been very terrible : However, to pacify 'em in some Shape, it was agreed, that every Man should have a Pint of Brandy *per* Day, which, by Calculation, would last 'em three Weeks. On this they seem'd very easy, and went to their respective Tents. The Captain told his Officers, that he would act nothing contrary to what was agreed on for the Welfare and
Safety

Safety of the Community. Finding the Captain in a Temper of Mind to hearken to Reafon, I faid to him, Sir, I think it my Duty to inform you, that I am not the Perfon whom you imagine to be the Principal in this Affair. The Captain anfwer'd, How can I think otherwife? I reply'd, Sir, the Paper I read to you was your Lieutenant's Projection: There fits the Gentleman, let him difown it, if he can. The Captain turning himfelf to the Lieutenant, fays, Mr. *Bulkeley* has honeftly clear'd himfelf. We then drank a Glafs of Wine, and took our Leaves. At Night the Captain fent for Mr. *Cummins* and me to fup with him; we were the only Officers prefent with him: When I was feated, I faid, Sir, I have my Character at Stake, for drawing back from your cock'd Piftol: Had I advanc'd, one of us muft have dropt. The Captain anfwer'd, *Bulkeley*, I do affure you, the Piftol was not defign'd for you, but for another; for I knew the Whole before. We then talk'd of indifferent Things, and fpent the Evening in a very affable Manner.

Saturday the 29th, came here five *Indian* Canoes, loaden with Mufcles; Men, Women and Children were about fifty: Thefe *Indians* had never been with us before; they
are

are not fo generous and good-natur'd as our
Friends I have already mention'd; they were
fo mercenary, that they would not part with
a fingle Mufcle without fomething in Ex-
change; their Stay was but fhort with us,
for the next Morning they launch'd their Canoes, and went off.

Tuefday, September the 1ft, the Carpenter
was fhot in the Thigh with feveral large
Pewter Sluggs by the Captain's Cook; but
he being at a great Diftance, the Sluggs did
not enter his Skin: Whether this was defign'd, or accidental, we don't know; however, we thought it proper to difarm him.

Wednefday the 2d, Wind at N. and N. by
W. with Rain. This Day we were inform'd
that three of the Deferters, *viz. James Mitchel,* Carpenter's Mate, *Joseph King* and
Owen Thomfon, Seamen, were gone over to
the Main in a Punt of their own building;
the others were here Yefterday, and I believe
would be gladly received again, but am of
Opinion there are few Voices in their Favour.

Friday the 4th, fome Diforders among the
People about watching the Provifions; fome
taking all Opportunities to rob the Stores.
Our Living now is very hard; Shell-fifh are
very

very scarce, and difficult to be had; the Sea-weeds are our greatest Support; we have found a Sort of Sea-weed, which we call *Dulse*; it is a narrow Weed, growing on Rocks in the Sea, which, when boil'd about two Hours, thickens the Water like Flower; this we esteem a good and wholesome Food.

Sunday the 6th, last Night the Store-Tent was robbed of Brandy and Flower: The People at hearing this were greatly enrag'd, and insisted on searching the Marines Tents; on Search they found four Bottles of Brandy, and four small Parcels of Flower. The Captain sent for the Lieutenant, Master, Gunner, Carpenter, and Surgeon, with Lieutenants *H——n*, *E——s*, and *F——g*, of the Army; Captain *P———n* was also sent for, but was so ill that he could not be present, but desir'd all might pass according to the Judgment of the above-mention'd Officers. A Consultation was held: Five of the accus'd Marines did not appear, dreading the Punishment due to their Crime; they march'd off to the Deserters: Four more, who staid to be try'd, receiv'd Sentence, on the first Opportunity, to carry them off to the Main, and there to shift for themselves with the former Deserters. The Seamen insisted on a

Pint

Pint of Brandy each Man *per Diem*, which was agreed on. The Provisions being found were put into the Store.

Monday the 7th, I was invited to a Dog-Feast at Mr. *J* ——*s*'s Tent: There were present at this Entertainment, the Lieutenant, the Honourable *John B* ——*n*, Mr. *Cummins*, Mr. *Cam bell*, Mr. *Young*, Lieutenants *Ewers* and *Fielding*, and Dr. *Oakley* of the Army. It was exceeding good Eating ; we thought no *English* Mutton preferable to it.

Tuesday the 8th, in the Afternoon, *William Harvey*, Quarter-Gunner, came to our Tent, with a Paper sign'd by seven People; the Contents as follow, *viz.*

THESE are to acquaint you, the Gentlemen, Officers, and Seamen of the Ship *Wager*, that, for the Easement of the Boat now building, we do agree to go in the Yawl, after she is fitted up, with allowing us our Share of Provisions, and other Conveniencies, to go in her to the Southward, through the *Streights of Magellan*, for the Coast of *Brazil.*

David Buckley, Quarter-Gunner
William Harvey, ditto

Richard

Richard Noble, Quarter-Mafter
William Moor, Captain's Cook
William Rofe, Quarter-Mafter
John Hayes, Seaman
John Bofman, ditto

The next Day, the above-mention'd added
one more to their Number, *viz. Peter Plaftow*, Captain's Steward : He came to acquaint
us, he was willing to go with them, and
hoped we would give our Confent ; we told
him we had nothing to do with it, therefore
he muft apply to the Captain.

Thurfday the 10th, hard Gales at W. N. W.
with Rain and Hail. The Captain fent for
the Lieutenant, Mafter, myfelf, the Carpenter, and Boatfwain : When we were all met,
the Captain afk'd us, if *Plaftow* had mention'd any Thing to us about going off in the
Yawl. We told him he had. *Plaftow* being fent
for, the Captain faid, *Peter !* I hear you are
for going in the Boat. He anfwer'd, Yes,
Sir ; I will take my Chance, for I want to
get to *England*. The Captain bade him be
gone for a Villain, and faid no more. This
Plaftow was a mighty Favourite with the
Captain, and had often been admitted to his
Converfation : He above all Men ought to
M have

have ftood ftedfaft to him, becaufe the Captain regarded him above the whole Body of
People, and hath been heard to fay as much.
It was this Day agreed, that the Sentence
put off on the 6th fhould be executed the
firft Opportunity, without any Delay; and
that no Boat fhould go off from hence before
all was ready, believing fome have a Defign
to go to the Northward.

Friday the 11th, Wind at N. N. W. The
People very uneafy; fcarce any Work done
for this Week paft; every Thing is at a
Stand; we have now among us no Command, Order, or Difcipline; add to our Uneafinefs, the Uncomfortablenefs of the Climate; we have been Inhabitants of this Ifland
fixteen Weeks, and have not feen ten fair
Days; the Murmurings of the People, the
Scarcity of Provifion, and the Severity of the
Weather, would really make a Man weary
of Life.

Monday the 14th, laft Night very hard
Gales at N. W. and W. N. W. with large
Showers of Hail, with Thunder. The Wind
To-day is much abated. As to the Article
of Provifions, nothing comes amifs; we eat
Dogs, Rats, and, in fhort, every Thing we
can come at.

Friday

Friday the 18th, *Dennis O'Lary* and *John Redwood*, Seamen, with six Marines, were put off to the Main, according to their Sentence; it being a fine Summer's Day. This Day the Lieutenant, bringing a Pair of Pistols to the Carpenter, and complaining they were in bad Order, did not imagine they were loaded, snapping the first it miss'd Fire, the second went off, but providentially did no Harm, tho' the Lieutenant had then a Crowd of People about him.

Sunday the 20th, little Wind, and clear Weather. Launch'd the Barge, and went off to the Wreck; we took up four Casks of Beef, with a Cask of Pease, which was stav'd; we serv'd out to each Man five Pieces of Beef, and Pease to such as would have 'em, but there were none to take 'em; having now Plenty of Meat, our Stomachs are become nice and dainty.

Wednesday the 23d, the People went to the Captain with a Two-Gallon Cagg, and ask'd it full of Wine: The Captain refus'd 'em; but apprehending that they would make no Ceremony of filling it without Leave, and carrying it off by Force, he thought proper to order it to be fill'd: They brought it to the Long-Boat, and drank it in her Hold.

Stept

Stept the Long-Boat's Maft forward. The People very much diforder'd in Liquor, and very quarrelfome.

Thurfday the 24th, I was fent on a Week's Cruize in the Barge; the Officers with me were Mr. *Jones* the Mate, and the Hon. Mr. B———*n* Midfhipman, and Mr. *Harvey* the Purfer, who was a good Draughtfman; we went in order to difcover the Coaft to the Southward, for the Safety of the Long-Boat; we were informed on our Return, that the People in our Abfence went to the Captain, and got two Gallons of Wine which they mixed with their half Pints of Brandy; they got all drunk and mad, but no great Mifchiefs enfued. Six *Indian* Canoes likewife came in our Abfence loaden with Men, Women, and Children; they brought with them Clams out of the Shells ftrung on Lines: The *Indian* Women dived for Mufcles, and brought them afhore in abundance; the Men went to the frefh Water River, and caught feveral Fifh like our *Englifh* Mullets. The People bought Dogs of the *Indians*, which they kill'd, and eat, efteeming the Flefh very good Food: The next Day the *Indians* went out and caught a vaft Quantity of Fifh out of a Pond, where they fent in their Dogs to hunt;

the

the Dogs dived, and drove the Fifh afhore in great Numbers, to one Part of the Pond, as if they had been drawn in a Seyne ; the *Indians* fold the Fifh to the People. This Method of catching Fifh, is, I believe, unknown any where elfe, and was very furprifing ; and, what is alfo very ftrange, after the *Indians* went away, we hauled the Seyne over the Pond, and could never get a Fifh.

Monday the 28th, returned with the Barge ; the firft Evening we were out we had a good Harbour for the Barge, which we put into ; the firft Animal we faw was a fine large Bitch big with Puppies ; we killed her ; we then roafted one Side and boiled the other, were exceedingly well pleafed with our Fare, fupped heartily, and flept well : The next Morning we got up at Day-breaking, and proceeded on our Cruize, finding all along the Coaft to be very dangerous ; at Evening put into a Place of very good Shelter for the Barge : Here we found the *Indians* had been very lately, the Shore being covered with the Offals of Seal : In an Hour's Time we killed ten wild Fowl ; we roafted three Geefe and two Ducks, the reft we put into a Sea Pye, fo that we fared moft elegantly ; got up at Day-light next Morning, but feeing the

Wea-

Weather hazy and dirty, thought it not proper to put out with the Barge, fearing we fhould not get a Harbour before Night; we took a Walk five Miles in the Country crofs the Land to the Southward, but could not fee any Shelter for the Boat, being then twelve Leagues from the Place we came from; fo we returned back in the Evening, and got into a fine fandy Bay; I think it as good a Harbour for Shipping as any I ever faw: Coming into this Bay, faw the Southmoft Land, which we had feen before, bearing about S. S. W. right over an Inlet of Land, about two Miles. After landing, lived as we did laft Night; in the Morning we walked over, where we found a deep Bay, it being eighteen Leagues deep, and twelve Leagues broad; here we had a very good Profpect of the Coaft; we found here the green Peafe that Sir *John Narborough* mentions in his Book.

Saturday the 3d of *October*, after our Return from the Cruize, the Lieutenant, the Mafter, myfelf, the Boatfwain, and Mr. *J*——*s* the Mate, went to the Captain, to acquaint him how forward the Boat was, and to confult fome Meafures to be obferv'd on Board the Boat, to prevent Mutiny; he defir'd a Day or two to confider of it.

On

On *Monday* the 5th, the Carpenter fent his Cafe Bottle, as ufual, to the Captain, to be filled with Wine; but it was fent back empty, with this Anfwer, I will give him none: This fudden Change of the Captain's Behaviour to the Carpenter, proceeded from fome Words which the latter dropt, and were carried to the Captain: The Words the Carpenter fpoke were to this Purport, That he was not to be led by Favour or Affeƈtion, nor to be biaffed by a Bottle of Brandy. To-day we heeled the Long-boat, and caulked the Star board Side, paid her Bottom with Wax, Tallow, and Soap that came out of the Ship.

Tuefday the 6th, hard Gales at N. W. and N. with Rain: This Morning the Lieutenant acquainted us of the Captain's Refolution, which was to be Captain as before, and to be governed by the Rules of the Navy, and to ftand or fall by them; it was objeƈted in the prefent Situation, the Rules of the Navy are not fufficient to direƈt us, feveral Rules being requifite in our Circumftances which are not mention'd there; that the whole Body of Officers and People are determin'd not to be govern'd by thofe Rules at prefent. This Objeƈtion was ftarted, not from a Difrefpeƈt

to

to thofe Rules; but we imagin'd, if Captain C——*p* was reftor'd to the abfolute Command he had before the Lofs of the *Wager*, that he would proceed again upon the fame Principles, never on any Exigence confult his Officers, but act arbitrarily, according to his Humour and Confidence of fuperior Knowledge: While he acts with Reafon, we will fupport his Command with our Lives; but fome Reftriction is neceffary for our own Prefervation. We think him a Gentleman worthy to have a limited Command, but too dangerous a Perfon to be trufted with an abfolute one. This Afternoon the People infifted to be ferv'd Brandy out of the Casks that were buried Under-ground; accordingly they were ferv'd half a Pint each Man. Got the Long-Boat upright.

Thurfday the 8th, this Day the Mafter went to the Captain concerning ten half Barrels of Powder more than can be carried off, which will make good Water-Casks for the Boats: The Captain told him not to ftart the Powder, or deftroy any Thing, without his Orders; and faid, he muft have Time to confider of it. In the Afternoon, Captain *P—mb—rt—n,* of the Land Forces, came on the Beach, and defired the Affiftance of the

Seamen

Seamen to take Captain *C—p* a Prifoner,
for the Death of Mr. *Cozens,* the Midfhipman ; telling us, he fhould be call'd to an
Account, if he did not. This Evening the
Carpenter went up to the Hill-Tent, fo
called from its Situation ; the People were
fhooting Balls at Marks ; fome of 'em were
firing in Vollies, without Shot or Sluggs :
One of the Men on the Beach fir'd at the
Tent while the Carpenter was in it, who
was ftanding with a Book in his Hand ; there
was a Piece of Beef hung clofe at his Cheek,
the Ball went through the Tent and the Beef,
but the Carpenter receiv'd no Damage. To-
day I over-haul'd the Powder, and told the
Lieutenant that I had twenty-three half Barrels in Store, and that we could not carry off
in the Veffel above fix half Barrels ; therefore purpofe to ftart the Overplus into the
Sea, and make Water-Casks of the half Barrels, they being very proper for that Purpofe. I defired him to acquaint the Captain
with my Intention ; that fince he had no Regard for the Publick Good, or to any Thing
that tended to promoting it, the Carpenter
and I had determin'd never to go near him
again. The Lieutenant declin'd going, fearing the Captain would murther him ; but he

N   fent

fent the Mafter to him, to let him know the Neceffity of ftarting the Powder: The Captain's Anfwer to the Mafter was, I defire you will not deftroy any one Thing without my Orders. We now are convinc'd the Captain hath no Intention of going to the Southward, notwithftanding he had lately given his Word and Honour that he would; therefore Captain *P—mb—rt—n,* in order to put an End to all future Obftructions, demanded our Affiftance to make him a Prifoner for the fhooting Mr. *Cozens,* intending to carry him as fuch to *England;* at the fame Time to confine Lieutenant *H———n* with him; which was readily agreed to by the whole Body. It was reckon'd dangerous to fuffer the Captain any longer to enjoy Liberty; therefore the Lieutenant, Gunner, Carpenter, and Mr. *J—s* the Mate, refolv'd next Morning to furprize him in his Bed.

Friday the 9th, this Morning went in a Body and furpriz'd the Captain in Bed, difarm'd him, and took every Thing out of his Tent. The Captain faid to the Seamen, What are you about? Where are my Officers? At which the Mafter, Gunner, Carpenter, and Boatfwain, went in. The Captain faid, Gentlemen, do you know what

you

you have done, or are about? He was anfwer'd, Yes, Sir; our Affiftance was demanded
by Captain *P———n,* to fecure you as a Prifoner for the Death of Mr. *Cozens*; and as
we are Subjeâs of *Great-Britain*, we are
oblig'd to take you as fuch to *England*. The
Captain faid, Gentlemen, Captain *P———n*
hath nothing to do with me; I am your
Commander ftill; I will fhew you my In-
ftruâions; which he did to the People; on
this we came out. He then call'd his Officers
a fecond Time, and faid, What is this for?
He was anfwer'd, as before, That Affiftance
was demanded by Captain *P———n* to take
him Prifoner for the Death of Mr. *Cozens*.
He ftill infifted, Captain *P—— n* has no Bufinefs with me; I could not think you would
ferve me fo. It was told him, Sir, it is your
own Fault; you have given yourfelf no manner of Concern, for the Publick Good, on
our going from hence; but have aâed quite
the Reverfe, or elfe been fo carelefs and
indifferent about it, as if we had no Commander; and if other Perfons had given themfelves no more Trouble and Concern than
you have, we fhould not be ready to go
from hence as long as Provifions lafted. The
Captain faid, Very well, Gentlemen, you have

caught

caught me Napping ; I do not fee any of you
in Liquor ; you are a Parcel of brave Fellows, but my Officers are Scoundrels: Then
turning himfelf to me, he faid, Gunner,
where's my Lieutenant ? Did not he Head
you ? I told him, No, Sir; but was here
to fee it executed, and is here now. One of
you (fays the Captain) call Mr. *B*———*s*.
When Mr. *B*——*s* came, he faid, What is
all this for, Sir? Sir, it is Captain *P*——*n*'s
Order. Captain *P*———*n* hath no Bufinefs
with me, and you will anfwer for it hereafter ; if I do not live to fee *England*, I hope
fome of my Friends will. On this the Lieutenant left him. The Captain then addrefs'd
himfelf to the Seamen, faying, My Lads, I
do not blame you; but it is the Villainy of
my Officers, which they will anfwer for hereafter. He then call'd Mr. *B*——*s* again,
and faid, Well, Sir, what do you defign to
do by me ? The Lieutenant anfwer'd, Sir,
your Officers have defign d the Purfer's Tent
for you. Hum ! I fhould be obliged to the
Gentlemen, if they would let me ftay in my
own Tent. The Lieutenant came to acquaint
the Officers of the Captain's Requeft; but they
judg'd it inconvenient ; as Mr. *H*——*n*'s Tent
join'd the Purfer's, one Guard might ferve
                                                    'em

'em both; accordingly all his Things were mov'd to the Purfer's Tent: As he was coming along, he faid, Gentlemen, you muft excufe my not pulling my Hat off, my Hands are confin'd. Well, Captain *B——s!* you will be call'd to an Account for this hereafter. The Boatfwain, after the Captain's Confinement, moft barbaroufly infulted him, reproaching him with ftriking him, faying, Then it was your Time; but now, G —d d— n you, it is mine. The Captain made no Reply but this, You are a Scoundrel for ufing a Gentleman ill when he is a Prifoner. When the Captain was a Prifoner, he declared, he never intended to go to the Southward, having more Honour than to turn his Back on his Enemies; and farther, he faid, Gentlemen, I do not want to go off in any of your Craft; for I never defign'd to go for *England*, and would rather chufe to be fhot by you; there is not a fingle Man on the Beach dare engage me; but this is what I fear'd.

It is very odd, that Capt. *C —p* fhould now declare, he never intended to go to the Southward, when he publickly gave his Word and Honour he would go that Way, or any Way where the Spirit of the People led: But he
after-

afterwards told his Officers, he knew he had a fevere Trial to go through, if ever he came to *England*; and as for thofe who liv'd to return to their Country, the only Favour he requefted from them, was to declare the Truth, without Favour or Prejudice; and this we promis'd faithfully to do: His Words, in this Refpeȼt, were as much regarded by us as the Words of a dying Man, and have been moft punȼtually obferv'd.

Saturday the 10th, little Wind at N. and N. W. Getting all ready for going off this Afternoon, the Captain fent for the Lieutenant and me, defiring us both to go to Captain ——*n*, to know what he intended to do with him. We accordingly came, and both promis'd to go direȼtly, and bring him his Anfwer. When we came out, went to the Lieutenant's Tent; from thence I expeȼted, and made no doubt, but he would go to Captain *P*——*n*'s: But when I ask'd him, he refus'd; which very much furpriz'd me. I thought it very ungenerous to trifle with Captain *C*——*p*, or any Gentleman in his unhappy Situation; therefore went alone to Captain *P*——*n*. When I deliver'd him Captain *C*——*p*'s Meffage, the Anfwer was, I defign, and muft carry him Prifoner to *England.*

England. I return'd, and acquainted Captain
C——*p* with Captain *P*——*n*'s Anſwer: He
ask'd me then, if the Lieutenant was with
me. I told him, No; and I believe did not
deſign it. He ſaid, Mr. *Bulkeley*, I am very
much oblig'd to you, and could not think
the Lieutenant would uſe me thus. In the
Evening the Lieutenant and I were ſent for
again: The Captain ſaid to the Lieutenant,
Sir, have you been with Captain *P*——*n?*
He anſwer'd, No, Sir. I thought, Sir, you
promis'd me you would: However, I have
his Anſwer from Mr. *Bulkeley*; I am to be
carried a Priſoner to *England.* Gentlemen, I
ſhall never live to ſee *England*, but die by
Inches in the Voyage; and it is ſurprizing to
me to think, what you can expeÊt by going
to the Southward, where there are ten thou-
ſand Difficulties to be encounter'd with: I
am ſorry ſo many brave Fellows ſhould be
led to go where they are not acquainted,
when, by going to the Northward, there is
the Iſland of *Chili*, not above ninety Leagues,
where we need not fear taking Prizes, and
may have a Chance to ſee the Commodore.
I made Anſwer, Sir, you have ſaid, that we
ſhall be call'd to an Account for this in *England:* I muſt tell you, for my Part, had I
been

been guilty of any Crime, and was fure of being hang'd for it in *England*, I would make it my Choice to go there, fooner than to the Northward : Have not you given your Word and Honour to go to the South-ward? It is true, there is a Chance in go-ing to the Northward, by delivering us from this unhappy Situation of Life to a worfe, *viz.* a *Spanifh* Prifon. The Captain faid no more but this, Gentlemen, I wifh you well and fafe to *England.*

Sunday the 11th, this Morning the Cap-tain fent for me, and told me, he had rather be fhot than carried off a Prifoner, and that he would.not go off with us; therefore de-fired me to ask the People to fuffer him to remain on the Ifland: The People readily agreed to his Requeft; and alfo confented to leave him all Things needful for his Support, as much as could be fpar'd. Lieutenant *H*——*n* and the Surgeon chofe to ftay with him. We offer'd him alfo the Barge and Yawl, if he could procure Men to go with him. The Queftion was propos'd before the whole Body; but they all cry'd aloud for *England*, and let him ftay and be d——n'd; does he want to carry us to a Prifon? There is not a Man will go. The Captain being
depriv'd

depriv'd of his Command in the Manner above-mention'd, and for the Reasons already given, it was resolv'd to draw some Articles to be sign'd for the Good of the Community, and to give the Lieutenant a limited Command. The Paper was drawn up in this Manner :

WHereas Captain *David C——p,* our Commander in his Majesty's hip the *Wager,* never consulted any of his Officers for the Safety and Preservation of the said Ship, and his Majesty's Subjects thereto belonging ; but several Times, since the unhappy Loss of the said Ship, he has been solicited in the most dutiful Manner, promising him at the same Time to support his Command with our Lives, desiring no more than to go off Heart in Hand from this Place to the Southward, which he gave his Word and Honour to do ; and being almost ready for sailing, did apply to him, some few Days past, to draw up some proper Articles, in order to suppress Mutiny, and other material Things, which were thought necessary to be agreed to before we went off ; but he, in the most scornful Manner, hath rejected every Thing propos'd for the Publick Good ; and

O   as

as he is now a Prifoner, and the Command given to the Lieutenant, upon his Approbation of the following Articles.

Firſt, As we have no Conveniency for dreſſing Proviſions on Board the Veſſel for a third Part of the Number to be carried off the Spot, therefore this Day ſerv'd out to every Man and Boy twelve Days Proviſion, for them to dreſs before we go off; and alſo it is agreed, that whoever is guilty of defrauding another of any Part of his Allowance, on ſufficient Proof thereof, the Perſon found guilty (without any Reſpect of Perſon) ſhall be put on Shore at the firſt convenient Place, and left there.

Secondly, In Regard to the Boats going off with us, we think proper to allow one Week's Proviſion for each Man appointed to go in them, in order to prevent Separation from each other, which would be of the worſt Conſeqence of any Thing that can happen to us; to prevent which, we do agree, that when Under-way they ſhall not ſeparate, but always keep within Musket-ſhot, and on no Pretence or Excuſe whatſoever go beyond that Reach. The Officer, or any other Perſon, that ſhall attempt a Separation, or exceed

ceed the above-mention'd Bounds, fhall, on Proof, be put on Shore, and left behind.

Thirdly, It is agreed, in order to fupprefs Mutiny, and prevent Broils and Quarrels on Board the Veffel, that no Man fhall threaten the Life of another, or offer Violence in any Shape ; the Offender, without any Refpect of Station or Quality, being found guilty, fhall be put on Shore, and left behind.

Fourthly, We do agree, whatever Fowl, Fifh, or Neceffaries of Life, we fhall happen to meet with in our Paffage, the fame fhall be divided among the whole; and if Captain *David C——p* fhall be put on Board a Prifoner, it fhall not be in the Lieutenant's Power to releafe him.

The aforefaid Articles were agreed to, and fign'd by the under-mention'd.

> *Robert Beans*, Lieutenant
> *Thomas Clark*, Mafter
> *John King*, Boatfwain
> *John Bulkeley*, Gunner
> *John Cummins*, Carpenter
> *Thomas Harvey*, Purfer
> *Robert Elliot*, Surgeon's Mate
> *John Jones*, Mafter's Mate
> *John Snow*, ditto

The

The Hon. *John Byron,* Midſhipman
Alexander Campbell, ditto
Iſaac Morris, ditto
Thomas Maclean, Cook
Richard Phipps, Boatſwain's Mate
John Mooring, ditto
Matthew Langley, Gunner's Mate
Guy Broadwater, Coxſwain
Samuel Stook, Seaman
Joſeph Clinch, ditto
John Duck, ditto
Peter Plaſtow, Captain's Steward
John Pitman, Butcher
David Buckley, Quarter-Gunner
Richard Noble, Quarter-Maſter
William Moore, Captain's Cook
George Smith, Seaman
Benjamin Smith, ditto
William Oram, Carpenter's Mate
John Hart, Joiner
John Boſman, Seaman
William Harvey, Quarter-Gunner
Richard Eaſt, Seaman
Samuel Cooper, ditto
Job Barns, ditto
James Butler, ditto
William Roſe, Quarter-Maſter
John Shoreham, Seaman

John Hayes, Seaman
Henry Stephens, ditto
William Callicutt, ditto
John Ruffel, Armourer
James Mac Cawle, Seaman
William Lane, ditto
James Roach, ditto
John George, ditto
John Young, Cooper
Mofes Lewis, Gunner's Mate
Nicholas Grifelham, Seaman.

Monday the 12th, at Day-light, launch'd the Long-Boat, and gave her the Name of the *Speedwell* (which God preferv'd to deliver us); we got all the Provifion on Board, and other Neceffaries. The Captain fent for the Lieutenant, myfelf, and the Carpenter, defiring us to leave him what could be fpar'd, and to fend to the Deferters to know if they will go in the Yawl to the Northward; we promis'd to grant him his Requeft. To-day every Body got on Board. The Captain, Surgeon, and Mr. *H——n*, had their Share of Provifions equal with us.

Tuefday the 13th, we fent the Barge to the Deferters, with Mr. *S——w* the Mate, to know if they were willing to tarry, and go

with

with the Captain to the Northward; to acquaint them what Provifion and Neceffaries fhould be allow'd 'em : They readily agreed to tarry.   On the Return of the Boat, deliver'd to the Captain the Share of Provifion for the Deferters, and fundry Neceffaries, as under-mention'd, *viz.*

> Six Hand-Grenadoes.
> Five half Barrels of Powder.
> Two Caggs of Musket-Balls.
> Lieutenant *H*——*n*'s Piftols and Gun.
> One Pair of Piftols for the Captain.
> Twelve Musket-Flints.
> Six Piftol-Flints.
> Sundry Carpenters Tools.
> Half a Pint of Sweet Oil.
> Two Swords of the Captain's own.
> Five Muskets.
> Twelve Piftol-Balls.
> One Bible.
> One Azimuth Compafs.
> One Quadrant.
> One *Gunter's* Scale.

Provifion deliver'd to the Captain, Surgeon, and Lieutenant *H*——*n*, with eight Deferters; which laft are to be at half Allowance of the Quantity made out to the

People,

People, which make the whole Number feven
at whole Allowance.

To the Captain, Surgeon, and Lieutenant
H———*n :*
  Six Pieces of Beef.
  Six Pieces of Pork.
  Flower ninety Pound.

For the Deferters :
  Eight Pieces of Beef.
  Eight Pieces of Pork.
  Flower one hundred Weight.

As foon as the above Things were deliver'd, we got ready for failing. I went and
took my Leave of the Captain : He repeated
his Injunction, That at my Return to *England*, I would impartially relate all Proceedings : He fpoke to me in the moft tender and
affectionate Manner; and, as a Token of his
Friendfhip and Regard for me, defir'd me to
accept of a Suit of his beft Wearing-Appa-
rel : At parting, he gave me his Hand with
a great deal of Chearfulnefs, wifhing me well
and fafe to *England.* This was the laft Time
I ever faw the unfortunate Captain *C*——*p.*
However, we hope to fee him again in *England,*

land, that Mr. *Cummins* and myfelf may be freed from, fome heavy Imputations to our Prejudice laid on us by the Gentleman who fucceeded him in Command, and who, having an Opportunity of arriving before us in *England,* not only in the Places he touch'd at Abroad, but at Home, has blacken'd us with the greateft Calumnies; and, by an imperfect Narrative, has not only traduc'd us, but made the whole Affair fo dark and myftical, that till the Captain's Arrival the L——s of the A——y will not decide for or againft us. But if that unfortunate Captain never returns to his Country, let us do fo much Juftice to his Character, to declare, that he was a Gentleman poffefs'd of many Virtues; he was an excellent Seaman himfelf, and lov'd a Seaman; as for perfonal Bravery, no Man had a larger Share of it; even when a Prifoner he preferv'd the Dignity of a Commander; no Misfortunes could difpirit or deject him, and Fear was a Weaknefs he was entirely a Stranger to; the Lofs of the Ship, was the Lofs of him; he knew how to govern while he was a Commander on Board; but when Things were brought to Confufion and Diforder, he thought to eftablifh his Command afhore by his Courage, and to

fupprefs

fupprefs the leaft Infult on his Authority on
the firft Occafion; an Inftance of this was
feen on the Boatfwain's firft appearing afhore;
fhooting Mr. *Cozens*, and treating him in the
Manner he did after his Confinement, was
highly refented by the People, who foon got
the Power in their own Hands, the Officers
only had the Name, and they were often
compell'd, for the Prefervation of their Lives,
to comply fometimes with their moft unreafonable Demands; and it is a Miracle, amidft
the Wildnefs and Diftraction of the People,
that there was no more Bloodfhed.

At Eleven in the Forenoon, the whole Body
of People embark'd, to the Number of
eighty-one Souls; fifty-nine on Board the
Veffel, on Board the Cutter twelve, and in
the Barge ten: At Noon got under Sail, the
Wind at N. W. by W. The Captain, Surgeon, and Mr. *H——n*, being on the Shore-
fide, we gave them three Cheers; which
they return'd. Coming out of *Wager's* Bay
fplit the Fore-fail, and very narrowly efcap'd
the Rocks; with the Affiftance of the Barge,
and our own Oars, tow'd her clear, and bore
away, into a large fandy Bay, on the South-
fide of the *Lagoon*, which we call'd by the
Name of the *Speedwell* Bay. At Four in the

After-

Afternoon anchor'd in ten Fathom fine Sand; the Barge and Cutter went afhore, there not being Room on Board the Boat to lodge the People.

Wednefday the 14th, frefh Gales at S. W. and W. with Rain. At Three this Afternoon, being fair Weather, weigh'd, and came to Sail to take a Cruize up the *Lagoon*, to try the Veffel; it being fmooth Water, fhe work'd very well; after three or four Trips return'd, and anchor'd where we came from.

THESE are to certify the Right Honourable the Lords Commiffioners for Executing the Office of Lord High Admiral of *Great-Britain*, That we, whofe Names are under-mention'd, do beg Leave to acquaint your Lordfhips, that Captain *David Cheap*, our late Commander in his Majefty's Ship *Wager*, having publickly declar'd, that he will never go off this Spot, at his own Requeft defires to be left behind; but Captain *Pemberton*, of his Majefty's Land Forces, having confined him a Prifoner for the Death of Mr. *Henry Cozens* Midfhipman, with Lieutenant *Hamilton* for breaking his Confinement, did infift on delivering them up on the Beach to the Charge of Lieutenant *Beans*; but

but he, with his Officers and People, confulting the ill Confequences that might attend carrying two Prifoners off in fo fmall a
Veffel, and for fo long and tedious a Paffage
as we are likely to have, and that they might
have Opportunities of acting fuch Things in
Secret as may prove deftructive to the whole
Body ; and alfo in Regard to the chief Article of Life, as the greateft Part of the People muft be oblig'd, at every Place we ftop,
to go on Shore in Search of Provifions, and
there being now no lefs than eighty-one Souls
in this fmall Veffel, which we hope to be deliver'd in ; we therefore, to prevent any Difficulties to be added to the unforefeen we
have to encounter with, think proper to
agree, and in order to prevent Murther, to
comply with Captain *David Cheap*'s Requeft :
The Surgeon alfo begs Leave to be left with
him. Dated on Board the *Speedwell* Schooner
in *Cheap*'s Bay, this 14th Day of *October*, 1741.

> *Robert Beans*, Lieutenant
> *Thomas Clark*, Mafter
> *John King*, Boatfwain
> *John Bulkeley*, Gunner
> *John Cummins*, Carpenter
> *Robert Elliot*, Surgeon's Mate

John

John Jones, Mafter's Mate
John Snow, ditto
Captain *Pemberton,* of his Majefty's
Land Forces
Vincent Oakley, Surgeon of ditto.

Thurfday the 15th, This Morning, it being
Calm, made a Signal for the Boats to come
off, by firing five Muskets. At Day-light
came to Sail, with the Wind at W. by N. It
blowing hard, and a great Swell, the Veffel
would not work; therefore we were oblig'd
to put into a fmall Bay, laying S. W. of
Harvey's Bay, where we had very good
Shelter, there being a large Ledge of Rocks
without us, which broke the Sea off. At
Eleven we fent the Barge to *Cheap*'s Bay for
what Canvafs could be found ferviceable,
having left a fufficient Quantity behind, to
fupply us with Sails, in Cafe we wanted 'em.
Went in the Barge the Hon. *John B——n,*
at his own Requeft, *Alexander C——l* Midfhipman, *William Harvey* Quarter-Gunner,
David Buckley ditto, *William Rofe* Quarter-
Mafter, *Richard Noble* ditto, *Peter Plaftow*
Captain's Steward, *Jofeph Clinch* Seaman, and
Rowland Cruffet Marine. This Afternoon the
Carpenter went afhore in the Cutter, with
feveral

feveral of the People, to look for Provender. Shot feveral Geefe, and other Sea Fowl.
Rainy Weather. Wind W. N. W.

Friday the 16th, continual Rain, and hard
Gales all Night at S. W. This Morning the
Carpenter came on Board, and acquainted us
that he faw an Anchor of feven Feet in the
Shank, the Palm of each Arm filed off juft
above the Crown: This Anchor we fuppofe
to have belong'd to fome fmall Veffel wreck'd
on the Coaft. The Cutter brought off Abundance of Shell-fifh ready drefs'd for the People.

Sunday the 18th, at Noon, the Cutter came
off, and brought aboard Plenty of Shell-fifh
and Greens. The Honourable Mr. *B* — *n*,
Mr. *C*——*l*, and three of the Barge's Crew,
came from where the Barge lay. Mr. *B*—*n*
came aboard, and inform'd us of the Barge's
being fafe in the Bay, where we left her, and
only waited the Opportunity of Weather to
come round with her: At the fame Time he
defired to know, if we would give him, and
thofe who would ftay with Captain *C*——*p*,
their Share of Provifions. This Queftion of
Mr. *B*——*n*'s very much furpriz'd us; and
what furpriz'd us more was, that he fhould
be influenc'd by Mr. *C*——*l*, a Perfon whom
he always held in Contempt. As for my
Part,

Part, I believe Mr. *B* —— *n* left us becaufe he could not get any Accommodation aboard the Veffel that he lik'd, being oblig'd to lie forward with the Men; as were alfo the Carpenter and myfelf, when below: It is very certain, that we are fo clofely·pent up for want of Room, that the worft Jail in *England* is a Palace to our prefent Situation.

Tuefday the 20th, ferv'd out to the People eight Days Flower, to be drefs'd afhore. I went in the Cutter to command in my Turn for a Week.

Wednefday the 21ft, clofe Weather; the Wind from W. to N. W. with Rain and Hail. Brought aboard Shell-fifh in Abundance. At Noon the Honourable Mr. *B* — *n* came with fome of the Crew Over-land; he ask'd me, whether the Boat's Crew were gone off, and if we had ferv'd the Provifion, for he wanted to return to the Barge. I told him all the People were out a Fifhing, and that the firft who came in fhould carry him off. On which he faid, I think we will go and get fome Fifh too, having nothing elfe to live on. This was the laft Time I ever faw his Honour. When the People return'd from fifhing, they told me Mr. *B* —— *n* had loft his Hat, the Wind blowing it off his Head.

I faid,

I faid, Rather than he fhould want a Hat, I
would give him my own. One of the Seamen forced a Hat on his Head; his Name
was *John Duck:* But Mr. *B——n* would by
no Means wear it; faying, *John!* I thank
you; if I accept of your Kindnefs, you muft
go bare-headed; and, I think, I can bear
Hardfhips as well as the beft of you, and
muft ufe myfelf to them. I took eight People, and went Over-land to the Place where
the Barge lay, to get the Canvafs that we
ftood fo much in Need of; but found fhe was
gone from thence. The People in the Barge
told our Men, that they would return to us
again; but it is plain they never intended it.

Thurfday the 22d, This Day we faw Sea-
Fowl in vaft Flocks flying to the Southward,
where was a dead Whale. Look'd out all
this Day for the Barge, but to no Purpofe.
The Barge not returning was a very great
Misfortune, having no Boat but the Cutter;
and if by an unlucky Accident we lofe her,
we muft be reduc'd to the greateft Extremi-
ties to get Provifion. The Perfons in the
Barge, except the Captain's Steward, always
approv'd of going to the Southward; but it
feems Mr. *C——l* the Patroon prevail'd on
'em to return to Captain *C——p.*

Friday

Friday the 23d, Saw Thoufands of Sea-Fowl; in the Morning they fly to the Northward, and in the Evening come back to the South; they are Birds of a very large Size, but of what Kind we do not know. Since we have been here we faw feveral *Indian* Graves; they are dug juft within the Surface of the Earth, with a Board on each Side, and a Crofs ftuck up at the Head. The Day following a Gun, a four Pounder, was feen near the Anchor in *Clam* Bay; we call it by this Name, becaufe of the vaft Quantities of this fort of Shell-fifh which are found there.

Monday the 26th, it being very calm, and fair Weather, I went afhore to bring off the People; weigh'd the Long-Boat, and took her in Tow over a Bar, where was ten Feet Water, but a great Swell; as foon as we got over the Bar, there fprung up a Breeze of Wind at N. W. fteer'd away S. half E for the Southmoft Part of Land, which bore S. by E. diftant fourteen Leagues. The two Points of Land make a large and deep fandy Bay; we founded, but found no Ground; it is a bald Shore clofe to. I kept a-head in the Cutter, in order to provide a Harbour for the Long-Boat; Providence directed us to a very good one: It blew fo hard, with thick hazy

hazy Weather, that we could not keep the
Sea. At Eight at Night we anchor'd in
eight Fathom Water, a-breaſt of a fine ſandy
Bay, and Land lock'd not above three Boats
Length from the Shores : At the Entrance of
the Harbour, which lies about a League up
the *Lagoon*, I ſet the Land; the Northmoſt
Point bore by the Compaſs N. by E. diſtant
twelve Leagues, and the Southmoſt S. by W.
diſtant five Leagues; the Entrance lies E.

Tueſday the 27th, Freſh Gales at W. and
cloudy Weather, with a great Swell without,
inſomuch that we could not put out to Sea;
we therefore ſent the People aſhore to dreſs
their Proviſions; each Man is allow'd but a
Quarter of a Pound of Flower *per* Day,
without any other Subſiſtence, but what Providence brings in our Way.

Thurſday the 29th, Early this Morning, it
being calm and thick Weather, with ſmall
Rain, we rowed out of the *Lagoon*; at Five
it cleared up, with a freſh Breeze at S.S.E.
ſteer'd S.W. and S.W. by W. ſaw a ſmall
Iſland bearing S. by W. the Southmoſt End
S. by E. This Iſland we call the Rock of
Dundee, it being much like that Iſland in the
Weſt-Indies, but not ſo large; it lieth about
four Leagues diſtant from the Southmoſt

Q   Point

Point of Land out at Sea. This Day it blow'd fo hard, that we were oblig'd to take the Cutter in Tow.

Friday the 30th, Hard Gales, and a great Sea; faw fome Iflands and fome funken Rocks; at Six faw the Main in two Points of Land, with a large Opening; on each Side the funken Rocks are innumerable; the Entrance is fo dangerous, that no Mortal would attempt it, unlefs his Cafe was defperate, as ours; we have nothing but Death before our Eyes in keeping the Sea, and the fame Profpect in running in with the Land: We ran in before the Wind to the Opening that appear'd between the two Points, the Northmoft of which bore N. by E. and the Southmoft S. by E. We fteer'd in E. and found the Opening to be a large *Lagoon*, on the Southmoft Side, running into a very good Harbour; here our fmall Veffel lay fecure in a Cove, which Nature had form'd like a Dock; we had no Occafion to let go an Anchor, but ran along-fide the Land, and made faft our Head and Stern. The People went afhore in Search of Provifion; here we found Plenty of Wood and Water, and fine large Mufcles in great Quantities. Serv'd to each Man half a Piece of Beef.

Saturday

Saturday the 31ft, This Morning caft loofe, and row'd towards the Mouth of the *Lagoons*, defigning to put out to Sea; but the Wind blew fo hard, that we were oblig'd to come to an Anchor. This Afternoon, in weighing the Grapenel, in order to go to the Cove, we found it foul among fome Rocks; all Hands haul'd, took a Turn round the Main-Maft, and went aft; which weigh'd the Grapenel, but ftreighten'd one of the Flukes: Here the Land is very high and fteep on each Side; the Carpenter and Cooper were on the higheft of thefe Hills, and found deep Ponds of Water on the Top of them; thefe Hills are very rocky, and there are great Falls of Water all along the Coaft: The whole Navy of *England* may lay with Safety in many of thofe *Lagoons*; but the Coaft is too dangerous for any Ship to fall in with the Land. The People To-day were very much afflicted with the Gripes, and Pains in their Side. Here are Abundance of Trees, not unlike our Yew-Trees; they are not above feven or eight Inches in Diameter, and the Bark is like Cedar. The Land is to Appearance very good; but on digging beneath the Surface, we find it almoft an entire Stone. We faw no People here, tho', it is plain, here have been fome

Q 2 lately,

lately, by their Wigg-whams or Huts. We are fo clofely pent up for want of Room, that our Lodging is very uncomfortable; the Stench of the Mens wet Cloaths make the Air we breathe naufeous to that Degree, that one would think it impoffible for a Man to live below. We came to fail, and fteer'd out of the *Lagoon* Weft; went into a fandy Bay, one League to the Southward of the *Lagoon*. *Indian* Huts to be feen, but no Natives.

Monday, *November* the 2d, at Five in the Morning, came to fail with the Wind at S. and S. by E. At Noon the Wind came to the W. and W. N. W. in fmall Breezes. This Day I had a very good Obfervation, it being the firft fince we left *Cheep*'s Ifland. We found ourfelves in the Latitude of 50 : 00 S. After obferving, bore away, and ran into a fine fmooth Paffage between the Ifland and the Main. Thefe Iflands I believe to be the fame that are taken Notice of in *Cook*'s Voyage. From the Entrance to the Northward, to the going out of the Cape of *Good Hope*, (as we call it) the Diftance is about fix Leagues, and the Depth of Water is from two Fathom to twelve; the Northmoft Land before we came into the Paffage bore N. by W.

and

and the Southmoft, or Cape of *Good Hope*
bore S. by E. In the Evening anchored in a
fine fandy Bay: Here we alfo faw *Indian*
Huts, but no People; To-day we fhot wild
Geefe in Abundance, and got of Shell-Fifh, as
Limpets and Mufcles.

Tuefday the 3d, at Four this Morning
weighed, and came to fail with the Wind at
W. till we got about the Cape of *Good-
Hope*, then at W. N. W. fteering S. and a
tumbling Sea from the W. The Cutter fteer'd
S. by E. into a deep Bay; fuppofing them
not to fee the Southmoft Land, we made the
Signal for her, by hoifting an Enfign at the
Topping-Lift; as the Cutter was coming up
to us, her fquare Sail fplitted; we offered to
take them in Tow, but they would not accept it; we lay with our Sails down fome time
before they would fhow any Signal of making
Sail; coming before the Wind, and a large
Sea, we ordered them to fteer away for the
Southmoft Point of Land after us, and to keep
as near us as poffible; but inftead of obferving our Directions, they fteered away into
the Cod of a deep Bay, fuppofed to be
King's Bay: The Cutter being much to Lee-
ward, and the Weather coming on very thick,
we were obliged to fteer after her, but foon
loft

loft Sight of her. The Place being exceeding dangerous, we could not venture any farther after the Cutter; therefore we hauled by the Wind to the Southward; it continued blowing hard, with thick Weather, with funken Rocks and Breakers, fo that we were obliged to bear away before the Wind into a large Bay, the Tide running rampant, and in a great Swell, every where furrounded with funken Rocks, that we thought nothing but a Miracle could fave us; at laft we got fafe into the Bay, and came to in two Fathom Water, we fteered in E. At Four this Morning rowed out between the Iflands; after we got out, had a frefh Breeze at N. W. fteered out S. S. W. then S. and S. by E. the Cutter a-head. At Seven in the Morning a-breaft of *Cape Good-Hope*, faw a large high Rock bearing S. fteered S. by E. going within it, and the Main a-breaft of the Rocks; faw a long Point making into Iflands bearing S. by E. fteer'd S. until a-breaft of them: The fame Day faw a very high Land, with a low Point running off, in fmall Hommacoes, bearing from the Northmoft Point S. by E. about eighteen Leagues; between thofe two Points, is a large deep Bay, all within furrounded with Rocks and fmall Iflands; fteered S. and S. by W for the outer-moft

moſt Point, the Cutter keeping within, and
we conſidering the ill Conſequence of being
embay'd, to prevent which we hauled the
Mainſail and Foreſail down, and kept the
Veſſel before the Wind ; at Eleven the Cutter
came a long-ſide, with her Mainſail ſplit ; we
called to them to take hold of a Towe-Rope,
but they refuſed, telling us that the Boat
would not bear towing, by reaſon of the Swell
of the Sea, therefore they would have us nearer
the Shore, where we ſhould have ſmooth
Water ; we anſwered them that the Water
was ſmoother without, and nothing nigh the
Sea that runs within ; beſides, we ſhall be
embay'd, therefore we deſire you to come on
board the Veſſel, and we'll take the Boat in
Tow : They had no Regard to what we ſaid ;
we at the ſame Time, for above a Quarter of
an Hour, lay in the Trough of the Sea, with
a fair Wind : The People in the Cutter would
neither make Sail, nor row ; at laſt, finding
them obſtinate, we hoiſted a ſkirt of the
Mainſail, and edged farther off, S. by W.
when they found we would not go into that
Bay, they hoiſted their Mainſail, and went
a-head ; being ſome Diſtance a-head, we
made ſail, the Cutter ſtill keeping a-head
till One o' Clock ; then ſhe bore away

S.

S. by E. and S. S. E the Reafon of which
we could not tell, it blowing very hard, with
a great Sea, nothing before us but Rocks and
Breakers, therefore of Confequence the farther in, the Sea muft be the greater. At
half an Hour paft Two, the Cutter, being on
the Beam, and four Miles within us, we bore
away after them; and in a very heavy Squall
of Wind and Rain we loft Sight of her: After
the Squall was over, it cleared up, but we
faw nothing of the Cutter, nor could we clear
the Shore to the Northward, being not above
two Miles off the Breakers; therefore we were
under a Neceffity of hauling to the Southward
for Self-prefervation, and very narrowly e-
fcaped clearing the Rocks: After running
about three Leagues, faw an Opening, where
we hoped to find a good Harbour; bore away
for the Opening; we were here again furrounded with Rocks and Breakers, with a
hard Gale of Wind, and a great Sea, the
oldeft Seaman on board never faw a more
difmal Profpect; we ran in before the Wind
for about two Leagues, expecting every Rife
and Fall of the Sea to be a Wreck, but Providence at length conducted us to an indifferent Place of Shelter: We are now in a moft
wretched Condition, having no Boat to go
afhore

aſhore in, to ſeek for Provender: And the greateſt Part of the People on board are ſo regardleſs of Life, that they really appear quite indifferent whether they ſhall live or die; and it is with much Intreaty that any of them can be prevailed on to come upon Deck, to aſſiſt for their Preſervation.

The People's Names in the Cutter are as follow, *viz.*

Names.	Quality.	Age.	Where born.
Thomas Harvey,	Purſer	25	*Weſtminſter*
John Mooring,	Boatſwain's Mate	34	*Goſport*
William Oram,	Carpenter's Crew	28	*Philadelphia*
Richard Phipps,	Boatſwain's Mate	30	*Briſtol*
Matthew Lively,	Gunner's Mate	34	*Exeter*
John George,	Seaman	22	*Wandſworth*
Nicholas Griſelham,	ditto	31	*Ipſwich*
James Stewart,	ditto	35	*Aberdeen*
James Roach,	ditto	21	*Cork*
James Butler,	ditto	32	*Dublin*
John Allen,	ditto	18	*Goſport*

Wedneſday the 4th, Hard Gales at W. N. W. and a great Sea without; ſerved out Flower and a Piece of Beef to two Men for a Week's Subſiſtence; the Weather is ſo bad that there is no other Food to be got.

R   *Thurſday*

Thurſday the 5th, Little Wind at S. W. with heavy Rains; at Six this Morning went under Sail, but could make no Hand of it, therefore were obliged to put back again: As ſoon as we came to an Anchor, the Boatſwain employed himſelf in making a Raft to get Aſhore with; this Raft was made with Oars and Water Barrels, when it was made, and over the Side it would carry three Men; but it was no ſooner put off from the Veſſel's Side but it canted, and obliged the People to ſwim for their Lives; the Boatſwain got hold of the Raft, and, with ſome Difficulty, reached the Shore; when he came off in the Evening, he informed us he had ſeen a Beef Puncheon, which gave us ſome Reaſon to apprehend ſome other Ship of the Squadron had ſuffered our Fate.

Friday the 6th, This Morning went under Sail, the Wind at W. N. W. with freſh Gales and heavy Rain; the Wind came to the Weſtward, and a great Sea, ſo that we could not turn out over the Bar: In our putting back we ſaw the Cutter, a very agreeable Sight, which gave us new Life; in the Evening anchored at the Place ſailed from; the Carpenter and others went Aſhore to get Shell-fiſh, which we ſtood in great Need of; at Night

Night the proper Boat's Crew would not go
Afhore with the Boat as ufual, but made
her faft a-ftern of the Veffel, with only two
Men in her, fhe never being left without
four before; at Eleven at Night one of the
Men came out of her into the Veffel, it
blowing very hard at N. N. E. in half an
Hour fhifted to N. W. and rainy Weather,
that we could not fee a Boat's Length: At
Two the next Morning the Cutter broke
loofe from the Stern of the Veffel; we called
from on board to *James Stewart*, the Man
that was in her, but he could not hear us; in
a fhort time we loft Sight of her, believing
fhe muft be ftove among the Rocks. The Lofs
of the Cutter gives the few thinking People
aboard a great deal of Uneafinefs; we have
feventy-two Men in the Veffel, and not above
fix of that Number that give themfelves the
leaft Concern for the Prefervation of their
Lives, but are rather the reverfe, being ripe
for Mutiny and Deftruction; this is a great
Affliction to the Lieutenant, myfelf, and the
Carpenter; we know not what to do to bring
them under any Command; they have troubled us to that Degree, that we are weary
of our Lives; therefore this Day we have
told the People, that, unlefs they alter their

Conduct,

Conduct, and fubject themfelves to Command, that we will leave them to themfelves, and take our Chance in this defolate Part of the Globe, rather than give ourfelves any farther Concern about fo many thoughtlefs Wretches : Divided the People into four Watches, to make more Room below. The People have promis'd to be under Government, and feem much eafier.

Sunday the 8th, This Morning the People requefted Provifions to be ferv'd ; it being four Days before the ufual Time, we think the Requeft very unreafonable. We laid the Inconveniencies before them of breaking in upon our Stores, confidering the Badnefs of the Weather, and the Length of our Paffage ; that if we are not exceedingly provident in Regard to ferving out Provifions, we muft all inevitably ftarve. They will not hearken to Reafon ; therefore we are obliged to comply with their Demands, and ferve out Provifions accordingly. Several of the People have defir'd to be put on Shore, defiring us to allow them fome few Neceffaries : We wanted to know what could induce them to requeft our putting them afhore in this remote and defolate Part of the World : They anfwer'd, they did not fear doing well, and
doubted

doubted not but to find the Cutter, which if they did, they would go back to the North-ward, otherwise they would make a Canoe; therefore infifted on going afhore. On their earneft Intreaties, the Body of People agreed to their Requeft: We haul'd the Boat clofe in Shore; the People who chofe to ftay behind were eleven in Number; we fupply'd them with proper Neceffaries, and they fign'd a Certificate, to inform the L—s of the A —y that they were not compell'd to ftay, but made it their own Choice, and that they did it for the Prefervation of themfelves and us.

A Copy of their Certificate.

THESE are to certify the Right Ho-nourable the Lords Commiffioners for Executing the Office of Lord High Admiral of *Great-Britain,* &c. That we, whofe Names are under-mention'd, fince the Misfortune of lofing the Cutter, have confider'd the ill Con-veniencies and Difficulties to be attended, where fo great a Number of People are to be carried off; therefore we have requefted, and defired the Officers and Company re-maining of the fame Veffel to put us on Shore, with fuch Neceffaries of Life as can be con-veniently

veniently fpar'd out of the Veffel. We, of our own free Will and Choice, do indemnify all Perfons from ever being call'd to an Account for putting us on Shore, or leaving us behind, contrary to our Inclinations. Witnefs our Hands, on Board the *Speedwell* Schooner, in the Latitude 50 : 40 S. this 8th Day of *November*, 1741. Which was fign'd by the following People, *viz.*

> *Matthew Langley*, Gunner's Mate
> *John Ruffel*, Armourer
> *George Smith*, Cook's Mate
> *William Callicutt*, Wafherman
> *John Williamfon*, Marine
> *John Mc Leod*, Boatfwain's Servant
> *John Hart*, Joiner
> *Jofeph Turner*, Captain's Servant
> *Luke Lyon*, Gunner's Servant
> *Richard Phipps*, Boatfwain's Mate
> *Henry Mortimer*, Marine

Witnefs,
> *John Cummins*, Carpenter
> *John Snow*, Mafters Mate
> *Vincent Oakley*, Surgeon of the Army.

Monday the 9th, at Ten at Night, we weigh'd, and row'd out of the Bay ; at Day-
light

light got about four Leagues right out, every
Way furrounded with Rocks and Breakers,
with a great Weftern Swell: We found it a
very difficult Matter to get clear of thofe
Rocks and Breakers; they reach along Shore
eighteen Leagues, and without us at Sea
eight Leagues; I take it, that from the Land
they are fourteen Leagues in the Offin; thofe
funken Rocks appear like a low level Land.
This Coaft is too dangerous for Shipping,
the Wind being three Parts of the Year to the
Weftward, which blows right on the Shore,
with a large weftern Swell, that feldom or
never ceafes; it always blows and rains; it is
worfe here than in the rainy Seafon on the
Coaft of *Guinea*; nor can we as yet diftinguifh Summer from Winter, only by the
Length of the Days. Steer'd out of the Bay
W. by N. then S. by W. then S. At Noon I
had a good Obfervation in the Latitude of
50: 50 South; the Northmoft Part of the Bay
bore N. E. by E. feven Leagues; the Southmoft Point of Land S. S. E. twelve Leagues.
This Coaft, as far as we have come, lies
N. by E. and S. by W. by the Compafs.

Tuefday the 10th, At Four this Morning
made all the Sail we could, fteering S. E. in
order to make the Land; at Six fteer'd in
E. S. E.

E. S. E. at Seven made the Land; at Eight
faw a Point of Land bearing S. E. diftant fix
Leagues, which, when a-breaft, feeing no
Land to the S. I take the Point for Cape
Victory, and the four Iflands we fee I believe
to be the Iflands of *Direction*, which Sir *John*
Narborough gives an Account of; excepting
the Diftance, they exactly anfwer his Defcription; therefore, by the Latitude in Yefterday's Obfervation, and by the Diftance we
have run fince, we are now at the Opening
of the *Streights of Magellan*. At Ten in the
Morning, hard Gales at N. W. fteer'd S. E.
the Cape bearing E. diftant four Leagues; at
Noon bore E. by N. diftant fix Leagues;
haul'd the Main-fail down, and went under a
Fore-fail. I never in my Life, in any Part
of the World, have feen fuch a Sea as runs
here; we expected every Wave to fwallow
us, and the Boat to founder. This Shore is
full of fmall Iflands, Rocks, and Breakers;
fo that we can't haul further to the Southward, for fear of endangering the Boat; we
are oblig'd to keep her right before the Sea.
At Five broach'd to, at which we all believ'd fhe would never rife again. We were
furrounded with Rocks, and fo near that a
Man might tofs a Bisket on 'em: We had
nothing

nothing but Death before our Eyes, and every Moment expected our Fate. It blew a Hurricane 'of Wind, with thick rainy Weather, that we could not fee twice the Boat's Length; we pray'd earneftly for its clearing up, for nothing elfe could fave us from perifhing; we no fooner ask'd for Light, but it was granted us from above. At the Weather's clearing up, we faw the Land on the North-Shore, with Iflands, Rocks, and Breakers all around us; we were obliged to put in among 'em for Shelter, finding it impoffible to keep the Sea; we were in with the Land amongft them, and compell'd to pufh thro', looking Death in the Face, and expecting every Sea to bury us; the boldeft Men among us were difmay'd, nor can we poffibly give an Account in what Manner we have been this Day deliver'd. After failing amidft Iflands, Rocks, and Breakers, for above a League, we got fafe into a good Harbour, furrounded with fmall Iflands, which kept the Sea off; here the Water was as fmooth as in a Mill-pond. We call this Harbour the *Port of God's Mercy*, efteeming our Prefervation this Day to be a Miracle. The moft abandon'd among us no longer doubt of an

S   Almighty

Almighty Being, and have promis'd to reform
their Lives.

Wednesday the 11th, The Wind much abated,
with Rain. This Morning weigh'd, and ran
farther in. In the Evening we faw two *Indians* lying on their Bellies on the Top of a
fteep Rock, juft over the Veffel, peeping with
their Heads over the Hill. As foon as we
difcover'd them, we made Motions to them
to come down; they then rofe up, and put
on their Heads white feather'd Caps; we
then hoifted a white Sheet for an Enfign; at
this they made a Noife, pronouncing *Orza,
Orza*; which we took for a Signal to come
afhore. We would not fuffer above two
Men to go afhore, and thofe difarm'd, left
we fhould put them in Fear. The *Indians*
had nothing in their Hands but a Club, like
to our Cricket-Batts, with which they kill
their Seal. As foon as they faw the two
Men come afhore, they walk'd away; and
when they perceiv'd our Men follow'd them,
and gain'd Ground of them, they took to
their Heels, frequently looking back, crying
Orza, Orza, beckoning the People to follow,
which they did for a Mile or two along
Shore, out of Sight of the Veffel : Then the
Indians fled to the Woods, ftill wanting our

People

People to follow them; but being difarm'd, they were apprehenfive the *Indians* would Bufh-fight them; fo they thought proper to give over the Purfuit, and to return to the Boat.

Thurfday the 12th, Hard Gales at W. N. W. with Rain. At Six this Morning we again faw the two *Indians*; they made the fame Noife and Motions to come afhore; at which I went with four of the People; the *Indians* walk'd and ran as before, looking back, and making Signs to follow, which we did till we got to the Place where the Canoe lay with four *Indians* in her. The two *Indians* got into the Canoe, and put her off the Shore before we could get nigh them; as foon as we got a-breaft of the Canoe, they made Signs as if they wanted Cloathing; we endeavour'd to make them underftand we wanted Fifh, and would truck with them; they had none, but fignified to us they would go and get fome : They had a mangey Dog, which they parted with to one of the People for a Pair of Cloth Trowzers; this Dog was foon kill'd, drefs'd, and devour'd.. Here we found Plenty of Mufcles, which gave us great Relief, having fcarce any Thing to fubfift on for this Week paft.

Friday

Friday the 13th, Very uncertain Weather, and fqually; the Wind variable from W.N.W. to S.S.W. This Morning all Hands afhore a fifhing. Lieutenant *E——rs* of the Marines kill'd a large Seal or Sea-Dog; it is exceeding good Food, and we judg'd it to have weigh'd feventeen Score.

Saturday the 14th, Little Wind at W.N.W. and clofe Weather, with Rain. At Five this Morning caft loofe, and fteer'd South out between the Iflands; the Weather clearing up, we faw the South Shore; it firft appear'd like a large Ifland, ftretching away to the Weftward, and at the Weft-End two Hommacoes like Sugar-loaves, and to the Southward of them a large Point of Rocks; fteer'd S.E. until the Point bore W. then fteer'd S. E. by E. I took the Point for Cape *Pillar*, and was fully affur'd of our being in the *Streights*.

Sunday the 15th, At Three this Morning caft loofe, and row'd, but could not get out, fo were oblig'd to put back, and make faft, it blowing hard, with thick Weather all Day; in the Evening it clear'd up. This Day feveral People drove a Trade with their Allowance, giving Silver Buckles for Flower, valued at twelve Shillings *per* Pound, and before Night it reach'd to a Guinea, the

People

People crying aloud for Provifions, which are now fo fcarce, that feveral on Board are actually ftarving through Want.

Monday the 16th, At Three this Morning caft loofe, being little Wind, and fteer'd up the *Streights* S. E. by E. the Wind at N. W. At Eight o'Clock got a-breaft of Cape *Monday*; at Nine the Cape bore W. diftant four Leagues; at Noon running along Shore, made two Openings, which put the reft of the Officers to a Stand, not knowing which to take for the right Paffage.   Asking my Opinion, I gave it for keeping on the E. S. E. Paffage, the other lying S. E. by S.   On which they faid, Sir *John Narborough* bids us keep the South Shore on Board.   I anfwer'd, That Sir *John* tells us E. S. E. is the direct Courfe from Cape *Pillar*; I'll venture my Life that we are now in the right Paffage; fo we kept on E. by S. half S.   After running a League or two up, and not feeing Cape *Quod*, nor any Outlet, the Wind blowing hard, we were for running no farther, whereas one League more would have convinc'd every Body; but they all gave it againft me, that we were not in the right Paffage : The Wind being at W. N. W. we could not turn back again; fo that we were oblig'd

to

to put into a Cove lying on the North Shore, where we found good anchoring in four Fathom Water; no Provifions to be got here, being a barren rocky Place, producing not any Thing for the Prefervation of Life. This Afternoon died *George Bateman,* a Boy, aged fixteen Years: This poor Creature ftarv'd, perifh'd, and died a Skeleton, for want of Food. There are feveral more in the fame miferable Condition, and who, without a fpeedy Relief, muft undergo the fame Fate.

Tuefday the 17th, At Five this Morning weigh'd, and row'd out, it being calm; at Seven a frefh Breeze right up the Sound; we could not turn to Windward not above a Mile from where we laft lay; we made faft along Side the Rocks; all Hands afhore a fifhing for Mufcles, Limpetts, and Clams; here we found thofe Shell-fifh in Abundance, which prov'd a very feafonable Relief. Juft before we got in, one of the Men gave a Guinea for a Pound of Flower, being all the Money he had.

Wednefday the 18th, The Wind at W N.W. in hard Squalls, with Hail and Snow. This Morning caft loofe, and ftood over to the Southward, believing the Tide to run ftronger and more true than on the North-fhore, hoping

ping

ping fhortly to get out of the Sound, which
is not above a League in the Wind's Eye. At
Two o'Clock got into a Cove on the South-
fide; made faft along Side of the Rocks; all
Hands on Shore getting Mufcles, and other
Fifh.

Thurfday the 19th, Frefh Gales at W.N.W:
with Hail and Snow. This Morning caft
loofe, and fail'd out, but could make no Hand
of it; our Boat will not work to Windward;
put back from whence we came, and fent
the People afhore to get Mufcles. This
Night departed this Life Mr. *Thomas Caple*,
Son of the late Lieutenant *Caple*, aged twelve
Years, who perifh'd for want of Food. There
was a Perfon on Board who had fome of the
Youth's Money, upwards of twenty Guineas,
with a Watch and Silver Cup. Thofe laft
the Boy was willing to fell for Flower; but
his Guardian told him, he would buy Cloaths
for him in the *Brazil.* The miferable Youth
cry'd, Sir, I fhall never live to fee the *Brazil*;
I am ftarving now, almoft ftarv'd to Death;
therefore, for G—d's Sake, give me my Silver Cup to get me fome Victuals, or buy
fome for me yourfelf. All his Prayers and
Intreaties to him were vain; but Heaven fent
Death to his Relief, and put a Period to his
Miferies

Miferies in an Inftant. Perfons who have not
experienc'd the Hardfhips we have met with,
will wonder how People can be fo inhuman
to fee their Fellow-Creatures ftarving before
their Faces, and afford 'em no Relief: But
Hunger is void of all Compaffion; every
Perfon was fo intent on the Prefervation of
his own Life, that he was regardlefs of·ano-
ther's, and the Bowels of Commiferation
were fhut up. We flip no Opportunity,
Day or Night, to enter into the fuppofed right
Streights, but can get no Ground. This Day
we ferv'd Flower and a Piece of Beef between two Men for a Week. Capt. *P—n*,
of his Majefty's Land Forces, gave two
Guineas for two Pounds of Flower; this
Flower was fold him by the Seamen, who
live on Mufcles. Many of the People eat
their Flower raw as foon as they are ferv'd
it. The Wind and Weather not permitting
us to go out, the Men were employ'd in getting Wood and Water.

Tuefday the 24th, This Morning, it being
calm, row'd out; at Eight o'Clock had the
fuppofed right *Streights* open, having a Breeze
at W. N. W. S. E. by E. through the firft
Reach, and S. S. E. through the fecond; then
faw three Iflands, the largeft of which lies
OD

on the North-fhore; and there is a **Paffage**
about two Miles broad between that and the
Iflands to the Southward; there is alfo another Paffage between that Ifland and the
North-fhore, of a Mile and a half broad.
Before you come to thofe Iflands there is a
Sound lying on the South-fhore: You can fee
no Sea-Paffage until you come clofe up with
the Ifland, and then the imaginary *Streights*
are not above two Miles broad. Steer'd a-
way for the Ifland S. E. about two Leagues;
then came into a narrow Paffage, not
above a Cable's Length over, which put us
all to a Stand, doubting of any farther Paffage. The Wind took us a-head, and the
Tide being fpent, we put into a fmall Cove,
and made faft. At Seven in the Evening,
being calm, caft loofe, being willing to fee
if there was any Opening; but, to our great
Misfortune, found none; which very much
furpriz'd us. The Lieutenant is of Opinion,
that we are in a *Lagoon* to the Northward of
the *Streights.* This I cannot believe; and
am pofitive, if ever there was fuch a Place
in the World as the *Streights of Magellan*, we
are now in them, and above thirty Leagues
up. If he, or any of the Officers, had given
themfelves the Trouble of coming upon Deck,

T   to

to have made proper Remarks, we had been free from all this Perplexity, and by this Time out of the *Streights* to the Northward. There is not an Officer aboard, except the Carpenter and myself, will keep the Deck a Moment longer than his Watch, or has any Regard to a Reckoning, or any Thing elfe. It is agreed to go back again.

Wednefday the 25th, Little Wind, with Rain. At Eight this Morning row'd out, and got about a League down; here we could get no Ground, and were oblig'd to put back again.

Thurfday the 26th, Little Wind; row'd out, got about five Leagues down. This Day we were in fuch want of Provifions, that we were forc'd to cut up the Seal-skin and broil it, notwithftanding it has lain about the Deck for this Fortnight.

Friday the 27th, Little Wind, and clofe Weather. This Morning caft loofe, and row'd down; had a frefh Breeze at North; fteer'd W. S. W. up into another Opening on the South-fhore, hoping to find a Paffage out of the *Lagoon*, as the Lieutenant calls it, into the right *Streights*. After going two Leagues up, faw there was no Opening; put back, and made faft, where we came from; being

deter-

determin'd to go back, and make Cape *Pillar*
a fecond Time; which is the South Entrance
of the *Streights.* Got Abundance of large
Mufcles, five or fix Inches long; a very great
Relief to us at prefent.

Sunday the 29th, Hard Gales from N. W.
to S. W. with heavy Rains. Great Uneafinefs among the People, many of them de-
fpairing of a Deliverance, and crying aloud
to ferve Provifions four Days before the
Time. Finding no Way to pacify them, we
were oblig'd to ferve them. We endeavour'd
to encourage and comfort them as much as
lay in our Power, and at length they feem'd
tolerably eafy.

Monday the 30th, Frefh Gales at W. with
continual Rain. This Day died three of our
People, *viz. Peter Delroy* Barber, *Thomas
Thorpe* and *Thomas Woodhead,* Marines; they
all perifh'd for want of Food: Several more
are in the fame Way, being not able to go
afhore for Provifions; and thofe who are well
can't get fufficient for themfelves; therefore
the Sick are left deftitute of all Relief. There
is one Thing to be taken Notice of in the
Death of thofe People, that fome Hours before they die, they are taken light-headed,

and

and fall a joking and laughing; and in this Humour they expire.

Tuesday, December the 1ft, 1741, Little Wind, and fair Weather; which is a kind of Prodigy in thofe Parts. In the Morning put out of the Cove, and got four Leagues down; then the Wind took us a-head, and we put into another Cove, where we got Mufcles and Limpetts. At Four this Afternoon faw an *Indian* Canoe coming over from the North-fhore; they landed two of their Men to Lee-ward of the Cove; they came oppofite to us, and view'd us; then went back, and came with the Canoe within a Cable's Length of our Boat, but no nearer; fo that we had no Opportunity to truck with them.

Wednefday the 2d, Little Wind, with Rain. At Nine this Morning row'd out, and got about a League farther down; the Wind be-ginning to blow frefh, we put into another Cove, and found Plenty of Shell-fifh, which kept up our Spirits greatly; for it is enough to dejeft any thinking Man, to fee that the Boat will not turn to Windward; being of fuch Length, and fwimming fo boyant upon the Water, that the Wind, when clofe haul'd, throws her quite to Leeward: We have been feventeen Days going feven or eight Leagues

to

to Windward, which muſt make our Paſſage very long and uncomfortable.

Friday the 4th, Little Wind at S. and fair. This Morning row'd out; at Ten got down, where we ſaw a Smoak, but no People; we ſaw a Dog running along Shore, and keeping Company with the Boat for above a Mile; we then put in, with a Deſign to ſhoot him; but he ſoon diſappointed us, by taking into the Woods. We put off again with a fine Breeze, ſteering N. W. by W. down the *Streights.* The Carpenter gave a Guinea this Day for a Pound of Flower, which he made into Cakes, and eat inſtantly. At Six in the Evening a-breaſt of Cape *Munday*; at Eight a-breaſt of Cape *Upright*, being fair Weather. Intend ⅃to keep under Sail all Night.

Saturday the 5th, Little Wind, and fair: At Four this Morning I ſaw Cape *Pillar*, bearing W. by N. diſtant eight Leagues; ſaw a Smoak on the South Shore, and at Noon we ſaw a Smoak on the North Shore, but we did not care to loſe Time: At Three o'Clock ſaw Cape *Deſſeada*, bearing from Cape *Pillar* S. W. diſtant four Leagues; at Four o'Clock wore the Boat, and ſteered E. S. E. The Lieutenant was now fully convinced

vinced we have been all along in the right *Streights*, and had we run but one League further, on *Monday, Nov.* 17, we had efcaped all this Trouble and Anxiety : As for my own Part, I was, very well affured, from the firft Entrance, that we were right; but the Lieutenant would not believe that it was Cape *Pillar* on the S: Shore coming into the *Streights*, but thought we were in a Lagoon to the Northward ; fo that we have been above a Fortnight coming back to rectify Miftakes, and to look at Cape *Pillar* a fecond Time : At Eight o'Clock came a-breaft of the Smoak feen in the Morning. The People being well affured that we are actually in the *Streights of Magellan*, are all alive. Wind at W. S. W.

Sunday, Little Wind at W. with Rain: At Three this Morning a-breaft of Cape *Munday* ; at Six a-breaft of Cape *de Quad* oppofite to which, on the South-fhore, faw a Smoak, on which, we went afhore to the *Indians*, who came out on a Point of Land, at the Entrance of a Cove, hollowing, and crying, *Bona ! Bona !* endeavouring to make us underftand that they were our Friends; when afhore, we traded with them for two Dogs, three Brant Geefe, and fome Seal; which Supply was very acceptable to us; we fupped on the Dogs, and thought them equal

in

in Goodnefs to the beft Mutton in *England:*
We took from the *Indians* a Canoe, made of
the Bark of Trees, but foon towed her under
Water, and were obliged to cut her loofe;
fteer'd N. E. by E. At Eight o'Clock a-
a-breaft of *St. Jerom's Sound*; at Twelve,
breaft of *Royal Ifland.*

The *Indians* we faw in the *Streights of
Magellan,* are People of a middle Stature,
and well-fhaped; their Complexion of a
tawney Olive Colour, their Hair exceeding
black, but not very long; they have round
Faces, and fmall Nofes, their Eyes little and
black; their Teeth are fmooth and even, and
clofe fet, of an incomparable Whitenefs;
they are very active in Body, and run with a
furprizing Agility; they wear on their Heads
white feathered Caps; their Bodies are covered with the Skins of Seals and Guianacoes:
The Women, as foon as they faw us, fled into
the Woods, fo that we can give no Defcription of them.

Monday the 7th, Frefh Gales at W. N. W.
and fine Weather; at Six this Morning a-
breaft of Cape *Forward,* fteered N. by E.
At Nine a-breaft of *Port Famen*; at Twelve
at Noon, put in at *Frefhwater-Bay,* and filled
one Cask of Water, having none aboard; at
One

One o'Clock put out again, fteer'd N. by E. expecting Plenty of Wood and Water at *Elizabeth's Ifland*; at Nine at Night paffed by *Sandy Point*; it bore S. S. E. and the Ifland *St. George* E. N. E. diftant three Leagues.

Tuefday the 8th, At Four this Morning, being calm, weighed, and rowed towards *Elizabeth's Ifland*, it bearing W. N. W. At Four in the Afternoon anchor'd off the Northmoft in eight Fathom Water, fine Sand, about half a Cable's Length from the Shore, put the Veffel in, and landed fome People to fee for Wood and Water: In the Evening the People came aboard, having been all over the Ifland in fearch of Wood and Water. but found none; here indeed we found Shaggs and Sea-Gulls in great Numbers, it being Breeding Time; we got a vaft Quantity of their Eggs, moft of them having young ones in the Shell: However, we beat them up all together, with a little Flower, and made a very rich Pudding. *Elizabeth's Ifland* is a beautiful Spot of Ground to Appearance, with very good Pafture; but it is intirely barren of any thing for the Support of Man. This Day *John Turner*, Marine, perifhed for want of Food.

Wednefday

Wednefday the 9th, At Four this Morning weighed, and fteered E. N. E. for the *Narrows*, with the Wind at S. S. W. when a-breaft of the *Sweepftakes-Foreland*, fteered S. S. E. on Purpofe to look for Water; after going along fhore about fix Leagues into a deep Bay, we faw a fine delightful Country: Here we faw the Guianacoes in great Numbers, ten or twelve in a Drove; they are to be feen in fuch Droves all along the Shore for feveral Leagues.

The Guianacoe is as large as any *Englifh* Deer, with a long Neck; his Head, Mouth, and Ears, refembling a Sheep; he has very long flender Legs, and is cloven-footed like a Deer, with a fhort bufhy Tail, of a reddifh Colour; his Back is covered with red Wool, pretty long; but down his Sides, and all the Belly Part, is white Wool: Thofe Guianacoes, though, at a Diftance, very much refembling the Female Deer, are probably the Sheep of this Country: They are exceeding nimble, of an exquifite quick Sight, very fhy, and difficult to be fhot; at Noon, finding neither Wood nor Water, wore to the Northward: At Three got a-breaft of the *Foreland*, hauled in for *Fifh Cove*, which lieth juft round the Eaftern Point; here we expe&ted to land, and

U   fhoot

fhoot fome of thofe Guianacoes; but when a-breaft of the *Cove*, the Wind blew fo hard right out, that we were obliged to bear a-way for the firft *Narrow*, it being impoffible to get in. At Eight this Evening entered the firft *Narrow*, meeting the Flood, which runs here very ftrong: At Twelve came to an Anchor in five Fathom, about a Mile off Shore: The Tide floweth on the Weftern Shore feven Hours, and ebbs five. This Day *Robert Vicars* Marine perifhed with Want.

Thurfday the 10th, At Four this Morning weighed, and came to Sail; at Six got out of the firft *Narrow*, hauled in for a deep Bay on the N. Shore to feek for Water: The Boatfwain fwam afhore, and in half an Hour afterwards came down on the Beach, and brought us the News of finding frefh Water: It being rocky Ground, and ebbing Water, the Veffel ftruck; we were oblig'd, in this Exigence, to flip the Cable, Time not permitting us to haul up the Anchor; we ftood off and on the Shore till half Flood; then went in, and took the Cable on Board: After landing fome People with Casks to fill, haul'd the Anchor up, and went about two Miles farther out.

Friday

Friday the 11th, At Three this Morning the Boat ftruck upon the Tide of Ebb; it ebbing fo faft, we could not get her off; in a Quarter of an Hour's Time the Boat was dry; we were favour'd with little Wind and fmooth Water, otherwife fhe muft have ftove to Pieces, the Ground being very foul; it ebbs dry above a League off, and there is Shoal Water a great deal further out; fo that it is dangerous for a Ship to haul into this Bay. While the Boat was dry, got all the Water-Casks out of the Hold, and put them afhore to be fill'd. At Six haul'd the Boat off, having receiv'd no Damage; at Eight, it being four Feet Flood, run the Boat clofe in Shore, and took off our Water, the whole Quantity being four Tons, out of which we were oblig'd to leave two Puncheons, one Quarter-Cask, with three Muskets, a Funnel, and fome other Neceffaries; and were very much concern'd, left we fhould alfo leave fome of the People afhore. The Wind blowing hard, and the Sea tumbling in, we were under a Neceffity of hauling off, and putting to Sea, for fear of lofing the Boat. Since we left the Ifland where the *Wager* was loft, we have feveral Times very narrowly efcap'd being made a Wreck, and fome Times have been

pre-

preferv'd when we have feen our Fate before
our Eyes, and every Moment expected it,
and when all the Conduct and Ability of
Men could have avail'd nothing. Any one,
who has been a Witnefs of thofe Providential
Deliverances, and doubts the Being of a Su-
preme Power, difqualifies himfelf from any
Title to all future Mercy, and juftly deferves
the Wrath of an incens'd Deity. This Day,
at Noon, being well out of the Bay, and
nigh Mid-channel over, fteer'd E. N. E. for
Cape *Virgin Mary*, with a fine Gale at S. W.
At One we faw the Cape bearing N. E. by E.
diftant nine Leagues; at Seven in the Evening
faw a low Point of flat Land, ftretching away
from the Cape S.S.E. two Leagues; at Eight,
little or no Wind, fteer'd E. by S. at Twelve
at Night doubled the Point, the Wind at W.
right in the Middle of the Bay, where we
fill'd the Water; in Land lie two Peaks,
exactly like Affes Ears. We would advife
all Veffels from hauling into this Bay, it being fhoal Water and foul Ground. As for
every other Part of the *Streights of Magellan*,
from Cape *Victory* to Cape *Virgin Mary*, we
recommend Sir *John Narborough*, who in his
Account is fo juft and exact, that we think it
is impoffible for any Man living to mend his
Works.

Works. We have been a Month in thofe *Streights*, from our firft Sight of Cape *Pillar* to Cape *Virgin Mary*. The whole Length of the *Streights*, the Reaches and Turnings included, is reckon'd one hundred and fixteen Leagues.

Saturday the 12th, Little Wind, and fair Weather. At One this Morning fteer'd N. by W. At Four the Wind came to N. W. Tack'd and ftood to the Weftward; the two Points ftretching off from the Cape bore N. W. by W. diftant two Leagues. At Noon, the Wind being at N. E. fteering along Shore from the Cape, faw on the Shore three Men, on Mules or Horfes, riding towards us; when they came a-breaft of us, they ftop'd and made Signals, waving their Hats, as tho' they wanted to fpeak with us; at which we edg'd clofe to the Shore, where we faw to the Number of twenty; five of them rode a-breaft, the others were on Foot, having a large Store of Cattle with them. On Sight of this, we anchor'd within a Mile of the Shore. The Cape bore W. S W. diftant feven Leagues; the Swell tumbling in from the Sea, would not permit us to fpeak with 'em; by their Motions, Actions, Cloathing, and by their whole Behaviour, we took them for Chriftians:

Chriftians : It being a plain level Land, they
rode backwards and forwards like Racers,
waving white Handkerchiefs, and making
Signs for us to go into a Bay, which lay about
a League to the Northward ; which we defign'd to do on the Tide of Ebb. The Flood
being very ftrong againft us, they waited on
the Shore till the Tide was fpent; we weigh'd
and ftood to Northward; the Wind blowing
right in from Sea, and a great *Swell*, we
could not clear the Land; fo that we wore
and ftood to the Southward, and very narrowly efcap'd clearing the Breakers off the
Pitch of the Cape, which lay about two
Leagues out at Sea to the Southward. **At**
Nine at Night the Cape bore W. diftant fix
Leagues; ftood out to Sea till Eleven o'Clock,
then wore and ftood in the Wind, fhifting to
N. N. E. The next Morning we fteer'd in
for the Bay, and faw thofe People again ;
but the Wind foon afterwards veering to the
Weftward, and blowing ftrong, we were
oblig'd to bear away : We could not by any
Means come to the Knowledge of thefe People ; whether they are unfortunate Creatures
that have been caft away, or whether they
are Inhabitants about the River *Gallegoes,* we
can't tell.

Tuefday

Tuefday the 15th, Frefh Gales, and fair Weather. This Morning faw the Land; the Southmoft Point bore W. S. W. the Northmoft Point N. N. E. At Eight faw two Ledges of Rocks, running two Leagues out from a Point of Land which makes like an old Caftle. At Noon the Extreams of the Land bore W. by N. diftant three Leagues; had a good Obfervation, Latitude 49 : 10 S. Courfe made this twenty-four Hours is N. by E. half E. diftant 104 Miles, Longitude in 74 : 05 W.

Wednefday the 16th, At Noon a-breaft of *Penguin* Ifland, not above half a Mile from Shore. We faw on this Ifland Seals and Penguins without Number, the Shore being entirely cover'd with them. We find the Penguin exactly to anfwer Sir *John Narborough's* Defcription; therefore we beg Leave to give it the Reader in that excellent Navigator's own Words. " The Penguin is a Fowl that " lives by catching and eating of Fifh, which " he dives for, and is very nimble in the " Water; he is as big as a Brant-Goofe, and " weighs near about eight Pounds; they " have no Wings, but flat Stumps like Fins; " their Coat is a downy ftumped Feather; " they are blackifh Grey on the Backs and " Heads,

" Heads, and White about their Necks and
" down their Bellies; they are ſhort-legg'd
" like a Gooſe, and ſtand upright like little
" Children in white Aprons, in Companies to-
" gether; they are full-neck'd, and headed
" and beaked like a Crow, only the Point of
" their Bill turns down a little; they will
" bite hard, but they are very tame, and
" will drive in Herds to your Boat-ſide like
" Sheep, and there you may knock 'em on
" the Head, all one after another; they will
" not make any great Haſte away." We
ſteer'd N. W. by N. for the Harbour of Port
Deſire: The going into this Harbour is very
remarkable; on the South-ſide lies one Mile
in the Land, an high peak'd-up Rock, much
like a Tower, looking as tho' it was a Work
of Art ſet up for a Land-mark to ſteer into this
Harbour; this Rock is forty Feet high. At
Five o'Clock got into the Harbour; run up
to *Seal* Iſland, which lieth about a League
up; here we kill'd more Seal in half an Hour,
than we could carry off, being oblig'd to leave
the greateſt Part of what we kill'd behind.
The People eating greedily of the Seal, were
ſeiz'd with violent Fevers and Pains in their
Heads. While we were at Port *Deſire* we
had Seal and Fowl in Abundance. The Carpenter

penter found here a Parcel of Bricks, fome
of 'em with Letters cut in them; on one of
thofe Bricks thefe Words were very plain and
legible, *viz. Capt. Straiton,* 16 *Cannons,* 1687.
Thofe we imagine have been laid here from
a Wreck. The Carpenter with fix Men went
in Search of Water; a Mile up the Water's
Side they found *Peckett*'s Well, mention'd in
Sir *John Narborough*'s Book; the Spring is
fo fmall, that it doth not give above thirty
Gallons *per* Day; but the Well being full,
fupplied us. The People grow very turbulent and uneafy, requiring Flower to be ferv'd
out; which, in our prefent Circumftances, is
a moft unreafonable Requeft; we have but
one Cask of Flower on Board, and a great
Diftance to run into the *Brazil,* and no other
Provifion in the Boat but the Seal we have
kill'd here: Nay, they carry their Demands
much higher, infifting that the Marine Officers,
and fuch People as cannot be affifting in
working the Boat, fhall have but half the
Allowance of the reft; accordingly they have
pitch'd upon twenty to be ferv'd half a Pound
of Flower each Man, and themfelves a Pound.
This Diftinction the Half-Pounders complain
of, and that twenty are felected to be ftarv'd.
While we were at Port *Defire,* one Day dref-

X   fing

fing our Victuals we fet Fire to the Grafs; inftantly the Flames fpread, and immediately we faw the whole Country in a Conflagration ; and the next Day, from the Wateringplace, we faw the Smoak at a Diftance; fo that then the Fire was not extinguifh'd.

Friday the 25th, Little Wind, and fair Weather, went up to our Slaughter-Houfe in *Seal* Ifland, and took on Board our Sea-ftore, which we compleated in half an Hour's Time; turn'd down the Harbour with the Tide of Ebb; in the Evening, the Wind at N. E. could make no Hand of it; fo bore away for the Harbour again, and came to an Anchor.

Saturday the 26th, at Three in the Morning, fail'd out of Port *Defire* Harbour; fteer'd out E. N. E. At Six *Penguin* Ifland bore S. by E. diftant fix Leagues, and Cape *Blanco* N. W. by N. four Leagues. This Day I took my Departure from Cape *Blanco*; I judge the Cape to lie in the Longitude of 71 : 00 W. from the Meridian of *London*.

Monday the 28th, Moderate Gales, and fair. This Day ferv'd out all the Flower in the Boat, at three Pound and half to each Man. We have now nothing to live on but Seal, and what Providence throws in our Way.

Friday,

Friday, *January* the 1ft, 1741-2, Frefh Gales, and fair Weather, with a great Sea. At Ten laft Night fhifting the Man at Helm, brought her by the Lee, broke the Boom, and loft a Seaman over-board. The greateft Part of our Seal taken in at Port *Defire,* for want of Salt to cure it there, now ftinks very much; but having nothing elfe we are oblig'd to eat it. We are now miferable beyond Defcription, having nothing to feed on ourfelves, and at the fame Time almoft eaten up with Vermin.

Wednefday the 6th, Departed this Life Mr. *Thomas Harvey,* the Purfer; he died a Skeleton for want of Food: This Gentleman probably was the firft Purfer, belonging to his Majefty's Service, that ever perifh'd with Hunger. We fee daily a great Number of Whales.

Sunday the 10th, This Day at Noon, in working the Bearings, and Diftance to Cape *St. Andrew,* do find myfelf not above thirteen Leagues diftant from the Land; therefore haul'd in N. W. to make it before Night. We faw To-day Abundance of Infects, particularly Butterflies and Horfe-ftingers. We have nothing to eat but fome ftinking Seal, and not above twenty out of the forty-three which

are

are now alive have even that; and fuch hath been our Condition for this Week paft; nor are we better off in Regard to Water, there not being above eighty Gallons aboard: Never were beheld a Parcel of more mife-rable Objects; there are not above fifteen of us healthy, (if People may be call'd healthy that are fcarce able to crawl.) I am reckon'd at prefent one of the ftrongeft Men in the Boat, yet can hardly ftand on my Legs ten Minutes together, nor even that fhort Space of Time without holding: Every Man of us hath had a new Coat of Skin from Head to Foot: We that are in the beft State of Health do all we can to encourage the reft. At Four this Afternoon we were almoft tranfported with Joy at the Sight of Land, (having feen no Land for fourteen Days before) the Ex-treams of which bore N. W. about feven Leagues; we ran in with it, and at Eight anchor'd in eight Fathom; fine Sand about a League from the Shore; the Northmoft Point bore about N. E. the Southmoft Point about S. W. by S. This Day perifh'd for want of Food Serjeant *Ringall.*

Monday the 11th, At Four this Morning weigh'd, and came to fail, fteering along Shore N. E. by E. This is a pleafant and de-lightful

lightful Country to fail by; we kept within
a Mile of the Shore; we faw Horfes and
large Dogs in great Numbers, the Shore being perfectly cover'd with them. At Noon
I had a good Obfervation in the Latitude of
38 : 40 S. At the fame Time faw a-head
Land, which I take for Cape *St. Andrew's*;
it is a long fandy Point, very low, where a
Shoal runs off S. E. about three Leagues.
Sounded, and had but two Fathom and half
at High-water. When we got clear of this,
we fteer'd N. E. into a fandy Bay, and anchor'd there in three Fathom and half, fine
Sand; the North Point bore N. N. W. the
South Point S. E. by E. Here is a great
Swell, and Shoal Water. This Bay we call
Shoalwater Bay.

Tuefday the 12th, Lying in *Shoalwater Bay*,
the Wind at S. E. and fair Weather. Having
nothing on Board the Veffel to eat, and but
one Cask of Water to drink, we put her in
as nigh as we could venture; fo that any Perfon, who had the leaft Skill in Swimming,
might get afhore: Here runs a pretty large
Surf, which may endanger our Veffel; this
puts us to a Stand: To go from hence without Meat or Drink is certain Death. A few
cf the healthieft were refolv'd to fwim on
Shore,

Shore, to get Water and Provifions; the Officers, *viz.* the Boatfwain, Carpenter, and Lieutenant *E ——rs*, to animate the reft, firft leap'd into the Water; eleven of the People follow'd them; in this Attempt one of the Marines was unfortunately drown'd: We tofs'd over-board four Quarter-Casks to fill with Water; lafhing to the Cask two Fire-locks on each Side, with Ammunition for fhooting. When the Officers and People got on Shore, they faw Thoufands of Horfes and Dogs; the Dogs are of a mongrel Breed, and very large. They alfo faw Abundance of Parrots and Seals on the Rocks but not a Bufh growing on the Place; they made a Fire with Horfe-dung, and fhot a great many Seal, which they cut up in Quarters to bring aboard. One of the Water-Casks being leaky, they cut it up, and converted it into Fuel to drefs the Seal. They caught four Armadilloes; they are much larger than our Hedge-hogs, and very like them; their Bodies are cafed all over with Shells, fhutting under one another like Shells of Armour. In this Country thirteen of his Majefty's *Britifh* Subjects put to Flight a thoufand *Spanifh* Horfe. Horfes are more numerous here, than Sheep are on the Plains in *Dorfet* and *Wiltfhire*. We on

Board

Board fee Abundance of Seal lying on the
Shore cut up in Pieces; but the Wind blows
fo hard we can by no Means get at it. We
think ourfelves now worfe off than ever, for
we are actually ftarving in the Sight of Plenty.
We have but two People on Board that can
fwim; to give them all the Affiftance we can,
the Lieutenant and myfelf, with the reft of the
People, propofed to haul the Veffel nearer in,
and make a Raft for one of the two to fwim
afhore on, and to carry a Line to haul fome
of the Seal a-board: With much Entreaty
thefe two Swimmers were prevail'd on to
caft Lots; the Lot falling on the weakeft of
'em, who was a young Lad about fifteen
Years of Age, and fcarce able to ftand, we
would not fuffer him to go. While our Brethren were regaling in the Fulnefs of Plenty
afhore, we aboard were oblig'd to ftrip the
Hatches of a Seal-skin, which has been for
fome Time nail'd on, and made ufe of for a
Tarpawlin; we burnt the Hair off the Skin,
and for want of any Thing elfe fell to chew-
ing the Seal-skin.

Wednefday the 13th, Fine Weather, and
calm. At Six this Morning the Boatfwain
fhot a Horfe, and the People a wild Dog.
The Horfe was branded on the Left Buttock
with thefe Letters AR. By this we conjecture

ture there are Inhabitants not far off. At
Nine veer'd the Boat in, lafh'd the Oars to the
Hatches, and made a Stage to haul up the
Seal. The People fwam off three Casks of
Water; fent on Shore one Quarter-Cask
more, and two Breakers. Came aboard the
Boatfwain, Carpenter, and Lieutenant *E—rs*;
and four Men more are getting the Seal and
the Horfe on Board; which was no fooner in
the Veffel, than a Sea-Breeze came in, and
blow'd fo hard, that we were oblig'd to
weigh; leaving afhore one Quarter-Cask,
two Breakers, and eight of the People. The
Wind at E. S. E. and a tumbling Sea, came
to an Anchor about a League off the Shore;
we fhar'd all the Provifions among the Company; we ftill fee the People afhore, but
can't get them off.

Thurfday the 14th, Hard Gales at E. S. E.
and fair Weather. Laft Night the Sea was
fo great, that it broke the Rudder-Head off;
we were doubtful every Moment cf the Veffel's parting, which if fhe had, we muft have
been all of us inevitably loft. We were oblig'd
to put to Sea, not being able to get the People
off. We fent afhore in a fcuttled Puncheon
fome wearing Apparel, four Muskets, with
Balls, Powder, Flints, Candles, and feveral
Neceffaries; and alfo a Letter to acquaint
them

them of the Danger we were in, and of the Impoffibility of our riding it out till they could get off.

In *Frefh-water Bay*, dated on Board the *Speed-well* Schooner, on the Coaft of *South America*, in the Latitude of 37 : 25 S. Longitude from the Meridian of *London*, 65 : 00 W. this 14th Day of *January*, 1741-2.

THESE are to certify the Right Honourable the Lords Commiffioners for Executing the Office of Lord High Admiral of *Great-Britain*, &c. That we, whofe Names are under-mention'd, having nothing left on Board the Veffel but one Quarter-Cask of Water, were oblig'd to put into the firft Place we could for Subfiftence, which was in *Frefh-water Bay* ; where we came to an Anchor, as near the Shore as we could, without endangering the Veffel, having no Boat aboard, and a large Surf on the Shore ; therefore Mr. *King* the Boatfwain, Mr. *Cummins* the Carpenter, and Lieutenant *E* —— *rs*, with eleven of the People, jump'd over-board, in order to fwim afhore, with three Casks for Water; in which Attempt *James Greenham* was drown'd in the Surf, off the Shore : The Sea-Breeze coming on, prevented the People getting on Board the fame Night; therefore, on *Wednefday* Morning, it being then calm, they brought to the Beach the Casks fill'd with Water, with Seal and other Provifions in great Quantities, which we haul'd on Board. The Boat-fwain, Carpenter, Lieut. *E—rs,* and three of the People fwam off; but the Sea-Breeze coming in, and the Surf rifing, the reft were difcourag'd from coming off; we haul'd a good Birth off the Shore, where we lay the Remainder of the Day, and all the Night. The Greatnefs of the Sea broke off our Rudder-Head, and we expefted every Minute the Veffel would founder at her Anchor. *Thurfday* Morning we faw no Probability of the People coming aboard; and the Wind coming out of the Sea, and not one Stick of Fire-wood in the Veffel to drefs our Victuals, and it being every Man's Opinion that we muft put to Sea or perifh, we got up a fcuttled Cask, and put into it all Manner of Neceffaries, with four fmall Arms lafh'd to the Cask, and a Letter to acquaint them of our Danger; which Cask we faw them receive, as alfo the Letter that was in it; they then fell on their Knees, and made Signals wifhing us well; at which we got under

Sail,

Sail, and left our Brethren, whofe Names are under-mention'd. Sign'd by

Robert Beans, Lieutenant
John King, Boatfwain
John Bulkeley, Gunner
Thomas Clark, Mafter
John Cummins, Carpenter
Robert Elliot, Surgeon's Mate
John Jones, Mafter's Mate
John Snow, ditto

The Names of the People left on Shore in the Lat. of 37 : 25 S. Long. 65 : 00 W.

Names.	Where born.
Guy Broadwater,	*Blackwall*
John Duck,	*London*
Samuel Cooper,	*Ipfwich*
Benjamin Smith,	*Southwark*
Jofeph Clinch,	ditto
John Allen,	*Gofport*
John Andrews,	*Manchefter*
Ifaac Morris,	*Topfham*

Thofe People had a good Profpect of getting Provifions, and we believe Inhabitants are not far off; they have all Neceffaries for

fhooting;

shooting; we hope to fee them again, but at prefent we leave 'em to the Care of Providence and the wide World. At Noon ʾfail'd hence; at Four in the Afternoon could not, clear the Land, and were oblig'd to anchor in five Fathom, two Leagues from the Shore; the Northmoft Point of Land bore N. E. by N. and the Southmoft Point S by W. Hard Gales at E. N. E. and a great Sea. At Noon Latitude in 38 : 00 S.

Friday the 15th, Frefh Gales at N. N. W. and a great Sea tumbling into the Bay. We are not able to ride it out; therefore, at Four in the Afternoon, got under Sail, and ftood off to Sea; the Southmoft Land bore S. W. by S. diftant five Leagues.

Monday the 18th, In the Latitude of 36 : 29 S. the North Point of *Frefh-water Bay* bearing S. W. diftant forty-four Leagues, we went to an Allowance of Water, at a Pint a Man *per* Day, having on Board not above twenty Gallons for thirty-three Souls.

Tuefday the 19th, Little Wind at S. and clear Weather. At Four this Morning faw Breakers right a-head; founded, and found five Fathom; faw the Land making like an Ifland, bearing N. E. by E. diftant twelve Leagues; fteer'd N. for about a Mile or

two;

two; fhoal'd the Water from two Fathom to
nine Feet; then fteer'd N. N. E. and deepen'd
the Water to five Fathom. By the Appearance of the Land, we are well up the River of
Plate, and do take the Breakers for the *Englifh* Bank. Steer'd and fail'd all Day E. N. E.
along Shore; in the Evening anchor'd in a
fine fandy Bay; faw two Men coming down
on Horfeback; the Boatfwain fwam afhore,
and got up behind one of them, and rode
away to their Caravans. When we made the
Land, we had not one Drop of Water on
Board : Several People fwam afhore to fill
Water; one of 'em, when afhore, drank
very plentifully of Water; in attempting to
come off, was fo weak, that he could not
reach the Veffel, but was unfortunately
drown'd. Got one Cask of Water aboard,
which reviv'd us exceedingly.

Wednefday the 20th, Mr. *Cummins* and myfelf went afhore; four of the Inhabitants
came down to us on Horfeback. As I could
talk *Portugueze*, I fell into Difcourfe with
them. They told me the *Englifh* were ftill
at War with the *Spaniards*; that they had
two fifty Gun Ships up the River of *Plate*,
and one fixty Gun Ship cruizing off Cape *St.
Mary's*; and not above fix Weeks ago a
feventy

feventy Gun Ship lying at Anchor, parted from her Anchors and drove on Shore; that the Ship was loft, and every Man perifh'd. They alfo told me they were *Spaniards, Caf-tilians,* and Fifhermen; that they came here a fifhing; the Fifh they took they falted and dried, then fold them at *Buenos Aires.* The Town they belong'd to, they call'd *Mount de Vidia,* two Days Journey from hence. I ask'd 'em how they came to live in the King of *Portugal*'s Land. They faid there were a great many *Spanifh* Settlements on this Side, and gave us an Invitation to their Caravan. We got up behind them, and rode about a Mile to it; where they entertain'd us with good Jurk-Beef, roafted and boil'd, with good white Bread. We fought to buy fome Provifions of 'em; but they had none but twenty-fix Loaves, about as big as Two-penny Loaves in *England*; which they would not part with under four Guineas. We be-ing in a weak Condition, fcarce able to ftand on our Legs, and without Bread for a long Time, gave them their Price. Their Patroon told us at the fame Time, if it fhould be known that they had fupplied us, they fhould be all hang'd. He promis'd, if we would give him a Fire-lock, he would get us fome

wild

wild Fowl, and as many Ducks in an Hour or two as would ferve all the People aboard. Mr. *Cummins* fent for his Fire-lock, and gave it him, with fome Powder and Sluggs. On our coming away, finding one of their Company miffing with a Horfe, we were apprehenfive of his being gone to betray us; therefore immediately went on Board, got our Water in, and made all ready for failing to the *Rio Grand.*

Thurfday the 21ft, little Wind at N. W. and fair Weather. At four this Morning got under Sail; fteer'd E. N. E. At Twelve faw low Land ftretch off to the Eaftward, which bore E. by S. At Four the Tide of Flood flowing ftrong in oblig'd us to come to an Anchor in a large Bay, in eight Fathom Water; the South Point bore S. S. W. the Eaft Point E. S. E. at Eight at Night got under Sail, fteering E. S. E.

Friday the 22d, Little Wind at N. and fair Weather. At Eight this Morning faw Cape *St. Mary's*, bearing N. W. diftant ten Leagues; at Noon it bore W. S. W. and the North Land S. E. by E.

Saturday 23d, Little Wind, and calm. In the Morning, not feeing the Land, fteer'd in N. at Noon faw Cape *St. Mary's*, bearing N. W. diftant ten Leagues; Latitude *per*
Obfer-

Obfervation 34 : 53 S. At Seven in the Evening, being in Shore and calm, anchored in
fourteen Fathom Water, fandy Ground; the
Cape.bearing W. by N. and the Northmoft
Land N. by E. This Day departed this Life
Mr. *Thomas Clark* the Mafter; as did alfo
his Son the Day following.

Sunday the 24th, The Wind at S and hazy
Weather. At Two in the Morning weighed
and came to fail; fteering N. E. within a
League of the Shore. At Three in the Afternoon faw three Iflands; the Northmoft of
which is the moft remarkable one I ever beheld, appearing like a Church with a lofty
Tower; at Four we faw three Iflands more,
fteer'd N Quarter W between thofe Iflands,
until we faw the main Land. The moft re_
markable of thefe Iflands is about four Miles
from the Main; They are all fteep. At
Eight anchor'd in fourteen Fathom, fine Sand.

Monday the 25th, A frefh Gale at E. N. E.
and cloudy Weather. At Nine this Morning
got under Sail, in Order to go back to thofe
Iflands to get fome Seal, there being great
Numbers on the Rocks, and we in great
Want of Provifion, with the Wind againft us.
We took the Opportunity of the Wind back
to the Iflands, but were difappointed, being
not

not able to get afhore for Provifions, came
to an Anchor in fourteen Fathom, fandy
Ground.   Hard Gales at N. N. E. with
Thunder, Lightning and Rain all Night.

Tuefday the 26th, This Morning, moderate
Gales at N W. and fair Weather, got under
Sail; after clear of the Iflands, fteer'd
N. E. by N. keeping along Shore; it is a fine
level Land, and regular Soundings fifteen Fathom, five Leagues off the Land. We have no
Seal, nor any other kind of Food on Board. We
have a fair Wind, and not far from our defir'd Port; fo that we are in pretty good Spirits.
This Day died the oldeft Man belonging to
us, *Thomas Maclean*, Cook, aged 82 Years.

Wednefday the 27th, Moderate Gales at W.
fteer'd N. and fail'd all Day within a Cable's length of the Shore in three Fathom
Water. We have now nothing but a little Water to fupport Nature. At Noon had
an Obfervation, Latitude in 32 : 40 South : I
reckon myfelf 18 Leagues from the *Rio Grand*,
and hope to fee it in the Morning.

Thurfday the 28th, Kept the Shore clofe
a-board, and founded every half Hour, not
caring to go within three Fathom, nor keep
without five, failing along by the Lead all
Night. At Six in the Morning faw the

Opening of the River *Grand*; kept with-
in the Breakers of the Bar, having at fome-
times not above feven Feet Water at half
Flood; fteer'd N. E. by E. until the River's
Mouth was fairly open; then fteer'd N. and
N. N. W. until a-breaft of the Town; an-
chor'd on the Eaft-fhore in two Fathom Wa-
ter. There prefently came a Boat from the
Shore, with a Serjeant of the Army, and one
Soldier. The Lieutenant, myfelf, and Mr.
Cummins, with Captain *P-——n* of the Land
Forces, went on Shore with them. The
Commandant, the Officers, and People of the
Place, receiv'd us in a moft tender and friend-
ly Manner. They inftantly fent on Board to
the People four Quarters of Beef, and two
Bags of *Farine* Bread. We were conducted
to the Surgeon's Houfe, the handfomeft Habitation in the Place; where we were moft
hofpitably entertain'd. At Four in the Afternoon the Governor came to Town; after a
ftrict Enquiry into our Misfortunes, and the
Reafons of our coming into this Port, being
fomewhat doubtful that we might be Infpec-
tors of their Coaft, he began to examine me,
the Lieutenant having reported me to him as
Pilot. He ask'd me if there was a Chart of
the Coaft on Board; and, if not, how it was
poffible

poffible we could hit the Bar, and venture into fo hazardous a Place as this is? I told him, as for a Chart, we had none of any kind; but I had a good Obfervation the Day before, that our Veffel drew but a fmall Draught of Water; that we kept the Lead always going, and in the Neceffity we were in, we were oblig'd, at all Events, to venture; and if we had not feen the Opening of the River before Night, we muft have been compell'd to run the Veffel afhore. He examin'd me alfo concerning the Places we ftopt at, from Cape *Virgin Mary* to this Port, and more particularly relating to the River *Plate.* He was very nice in his Enquiry of our putting in at Cape *St. Mary's,* and of the Bearings and Diftance along Shore from thence to this Port. When he throughly fatisfy'd himfelf, he embraced us, and bleft himfelf to think of our Deliverance, which he term'd a Miracle. He offer'd every Thing the Country could afford to our Relief; the Sick were order'd to be taken Care of in the Hofpital: He took the Lieutenant and the Land Officers home with him; and defired the Commandant to fee that the reft of the Officers and People wanted for nothing. Before he went he inform'd us, that his Majefty's Ships

the

the *Severn* and *Pearl* were at *Rio Janeiro*, in great Diftrefs; that they had fent to *England* for Men, and could nat fail from thence until the Arrival of the *Flota*, which would be in *May* or *June*. He alfo told us, that we fhould be difpatch'd in the firft Veffel which arriv'd in this Port; for he did not think we could with Safety go any farther in our own; and that there could not be found twelve Seamen in the *Brasils* that would venture over the Bar in her to fail to *Rio Janeiro*; therefore he order'd our little *Speedwell* afhore; this Wonder the People are continually flocking to fee; and it is now about nine Months fince we were caft away in the *Wager*; in which Time, I believe, no Mortals have experienc'd more Difficulties and Miferies than we have. This Day may be juftly ftiled the Day of our Deliverance, and ought to be remember'd accordingly.

Sunday the 31ft, Little or nothing remarkable fince the Day we came in, only a wonderful Change in our Diet; we live on the beft the Country can produce, and have Plenty of every Thing. This Afternoon the Governor, Commandant, and Commiffary, came on Board, to fee our little *Speedwell*; they were furpriz'd, that thirty Souls, the

Number

Number of People now living, could be
ftow'd in fo fmall a Veffel; but that fhe could
contain the Number which firft embark'd
with us, was to them amazing, and beyond
all Belief: They could not conceive how the
Man at Helm could fteer without falling
over-board, there not being above four Inches
Rife from the Deck. I told them he fat
down, and clap'd his Feet againft the Rife;
and fhow'd them in what Manner we fecured
ourfelves. The Governor, after viewing the
Veffel over, told us, we were more welcome
to him in the miferable Condition we arriv'd,
than if we had brought all the Wealth in the
World with us. At the fame Time he fully
affur'd us, we fhould be fupply'd with every
Thing that the Country could afford; that he
would difpatch us the firft Opportunity to
Rio Janeiro; and whenever we ftood in Need
of any Thing, he order'd us to acquaint the
Commandant, and our Wants fhould be inftantly fupply'd. He then took Leave of us,
and wifh'd us well All the Deference and
dutiful Refpect we could fhow him, to exprefs a grateful Senfe of his Favour, was by
manning the Veffel, and giving him three
Cheers. The next Day arriv'd at this Place
the Brigadier-Governor of the Ifland St. *Ca-*
tharine;

tharine; he came clofe by our Veffel, we mann'd her, and gave him three Cheers. The Soldiers of the Garrifon, having twenty Months Arrears due to them, expected the Brigadier was come to pay them ; but when they found themfelves difappointed, they made a great Difturbance among themfelves. I apply'd to the Commandant for a Houfe, the Veffel, in rainy Weather, not being fit to lie in; he order'd me one joining to his own, and gave me the Key.   I took with me Mr. *Cummins*, Mr. *Jones*, Mr. *Snow*, Mr. *Oakley*, and the Cooper; we brought our trifling Neceffaries on Shore, and remov'd to our new Habitation : Here we were dry and warm ; and tho' we had no Bedding, we lodg'd very comfortably.   Since the Lofs of the *Wager*, we have been ufed to lie hard ; at prefent we think ourfelves very happily fix'd, and heartily wifh that all the Perfons who furviv'd the Lofs of the Ship were in fo good a Situation as ourfelves.

Tuefday, February the 2d, 1741-2, Great Murmurings among the Soldiers ; they detain'd the Brigadier from going back, as he intended, this Morning, till he promis'd to difpatch the Money, Cloaths, and Provifions, and to fee their Grievances adjufted.   On
thofe

thofe Terms they have agreed he fhall go;
and this Evening he return'd for St. *Catha-*
rine's. We apprehended, till now, that the
right Officers were in Place; but we find
ourfelves miftaken. Some Time before we
arrived here, there was an Infurrection among
the Soldiers: Their Defign was againft the
Governor; but by his Addrefs, and fair Pro-
mifes of feeing them righted, he diverted the
Storm from himfelf, and got himfelf continued in his Station; as were alfo the Major
and Commiffary. The Soldiers difmifs'd the
reft of the Officers, and fupply'd their Places
with their own People, tho' they were lately
private Men; they appear'd very grand, and
were not diftinguifh'd in Drefs from the proper Officers. The Difturbance at *Rio Grand*
is of no Service to us, for we feel the Effects
of it; our Allowance is now fo fmall that it
will hardly fupport Nature; the People have
been without *Farina*, which is their Bread,
for fome Days paft. We apply'd to the Governor, who promis'd to fupply us the next
Day; accordingly we went for a Supply,
which created frefh Murmurings among the
Soldiers; however we got a fmall Quantity
of Bread to fupply us for ten Days. The
Store-keeper fhow'd me all the Provifions,
which,

which, confidering there were a thoufand to draw their Subfiftence from it, was a fmall Stock indeed, and not above fix Weeks at the prefent Allowance. He told me we were ferv'd equally with the Soldiers; and when more Stores came, which they fhortly expected, our Allowance fhould be encreas'd. I think, in Reafon, this is as much as we can expect. The Lieutenant not coming nigh us fince our firft landing, I went with the People up to him at the Governor's, about two Miles from this Port, to endeavour to prevail with him to get us difpatch'd, acquainting him of the Call and Neceffity there was for our Affiftance on Board the two diftrefs'd Ships at *Rio Janeiro.* He faid he had fpoke to the Governor, and could not get us difpatch'd till another Veffel came in. I told him, as the Garrifon were in want of Provifions, what we were living on here, would carry us off; and if any Misfortune fhould attend the·Veffel expected in with the Provifions, we fhould be put very hard to it for a Subfiftence. He promis'd to acquaint the Governor; on which I took my Leave.

February the 17th, This Evening came into this Garrifon three Seamen, giving an Account of their belonging to a Veffel with Provi-

Provifions and Stores for this Place, from *Rio Janeiro*; that they had been from thence three Months, and had been off the Bar waiting an Opportunity to come in; that not having any frefh Water aboard, they were oblig'd to come to an Anchor ten Leagues to the Southward of this Port; that a Canoe was fent with thofe three Men to fill the Water, but the Wind coming in from the Sea, and blowing hard, oblig'd the Veffel to put to Sea, and leave them afhore, from whence they travelled here, and believ'd the Veffel was gone to St. *Catharine's*. The Governor, not fatisfy'd with their Report, took them for Spies, and kept them as fuch. However, in a Day or two afterwards, he difpatch'd a Pilot and two Seamen for the Ifland St. *Catharine*, to bring the Veffel round, in Cafe fhe fhould be there.

I took this Opportunity of fending a Letter by them to the Honourable Capt. *Murray*, Commander of his Majefty's Ship the *Pearl*, at *Rio Janeiro*; defiring them to order it to be difpatch'd by the firft Ship from St. *Catharine's* to the *Rio Janeiro*.

Honourable Sir,

I Take it as a Duty incumbent on me to acquaint you, that his Majefty's Ship the

Wager

Wager was wreck'd on a defolate Ifland on the Coaft of *Patagonia*, in the Latitude of 47 : 00 S. and W. Longitude from the Meridian of *London* 81 : 30, on the 14th of *May*, 1741. After lengthning the Long-Boat, and fitting her in the beft Manner we could, launch'd her on the 13th of *October*, and embark'd and fail'd on the 14th, with the Barge and Cutter, to the Number of eighty-one Souls in all. Capt. *Cheep* —, at his own Requeft, tarried behind, with Lieutenant *Hamilton*, and Mr. *Elliot* the Surgeon. After a long and fatiguing Paffage, coming through the *Streights of Magellan*, we arrived here the 28th of *January*, 1741-2; bringing into this Port alive to the Number of thirty, *viz.*

> *Robert Beans*, Lieutenant
> *John Bulkeley*, Gunner
> *John Cummins*, Carpenter
> *Robert Elliot*, Surgeon's Mate
> *John Jones*, Mafter's Mate
> *John Snow*, ditto
> *John Mooring*, Boatfwain's Mate
> *John Young*, Cooper
> *William Oram*, Carpenter's Crew
> *John King*, Boatfwain
> *Nicholas Grifelham*, Seaman
> *Samuel Stook*, ditto

James

James Mac Cawle, Seaman
William Lane, ditto
John Montgomery, ditto
John George, ditto
Richard Eaſt, ditto
James Butler, ditto
John Pitman, ditto
Job Barns, ditto
John Shoreham, ditto
Thomas Edmunds, ditto
Richard Powell, ditto
Diego Findall, (the *Portugueze* Boy)

Capt. *Robert Pemberton,* of his Majeſty's
    Land Forces
Lieutenants *Ewers* and *Fielding,* ditto
Vincent Oakley, Surgeon of ditto
And two Marines

All which are living at preſent, and waiting
an Opportunity of a Paſſage in a *Portugueze*
Veſſel, our own not being in a Condition to
proceed any farther, having no Sails, and being
ſo bad in all other Reſpeſts, that the Governor will not ſuffer us to hazard our Lives in
her; but hath promis'd to diſpatch us in the
very firſt Veſſel that arrives in this Port;
where we, with Impatience, are oblig'd to

tarry.

tarry. We humbly pay our Duty to Capt. *Leg*, praying the Reprefentation of this to him. From,

Moſt Honourable Sir,

Yours, &c.

Saturday the 20th, Laſt Night the three Seamen which came here, as mention'd before, with five more of this Place, attempted to run away with one of the large Boats; but they were purfu'd and taken: Their Defign was for the River *Plate*, the Wind then favouring them. This is evident, that the Governor was right in his Conjecture, and did not fufpect them wrongfully; they are now Prifoners in the Guard-Houfe. The next Morning I went to the Lieutenant, defiring him to apply to the Governor for a Pafs and Horfes for myfelf, Mr. *Cummins*, and *John Young*, to go by Land to St. *Catharine*'s and St. *Francifco*; where we need not doubt of a Paffage to his Majefty's diftrefs'd Ships at *Rio Janeiro*: That it was our Duty to haften to their Affiftance: That he, the Lieutenant, ought, the very Day after our Arrival into this Port, without any Regard
to

to Expence and Charges, to have difpatch'd
a fpecial Meffenger by Land; and then we
might have been affured of a Veffel before
now. The Lieutenant anfwer'd, he had a
Thought of enquiring at firft coming about
what I had mention'd, and of going himfelf,
tho' it coft him fifty Pounds; but he was inform'd it was impoffible to go by Land. I
ask'd him, if fo, how came the Brigadier
from St. *Catharine*'s here? And how do People weekly go from hence tIPther? As for
Fatigue or Trouble, whoever undertook to
go, he muft expect that; but there was no
Hardfhip to be encounter'd comparable to
what we had already undergone. We lay
here on Expence to the King, without doing
any Service, and run the Hazard of not only
lofing the Opportunity of getting on Board
our own Ships, but perhaps of miffing the
Flota, and of wintering here; therefore I
beg'd he would entreat the Governor to let
us have Horfes and Guides; which he promis'd to mention to the Governor at Dinner,
and fend me his Anfwer in the Afternoon
without fail. I waited with Impatience for
this Anfwer; but the Lieutenant failing in
his Promife, was the Occafion of my fending
him this Letter.

S I R,

S I R,

I Am sorry you should give me the Liberty of telling you, you have not discharg'd your Promise, by letting us know the Governor's Answer to what we requested: Which was, at our Expence and Charge, to go to the Assistance of his Majesty's Ships at *Rio Janeiro*; since which Time I am to inform you that we are in want of Provision, having none of any kind allow'd us yesterday, and but one small Fish *per* Man for two Days before. The Meaning of which I believe is owing to you, by the endeavouring, through the Persuasions of the Persons you confide in, to blacken us, and in so vile a Manner, that you seem unacquainted with the ill Consequence, which may attend the touching a Man's Character We know, and are fully convinced, from what has been done already, that nothing will be allow'd or granted us but by your Means: Mr. *Cummins* and myself ask no Favour from you, but to use your Endeavours to get us Dispatches to the Ships at *Rio Janeiro*, where every Man must give Account of his Actions, and Justice take Place. If I am not mistaken, you told me that what we were supply'd with here, was a Bounty flowing from the

generous

generous Spirit of the Governor, and the Gentlemen of the Place. If this be the Cafe, we ought to be very thankful indeed. I am furprized, Sir, you don't fee the Grievances of the Inhabitants here, and hear the Soldiers Murmurings for want of their Arrears. If they fhould revolt at this Juncture, we fhall ftand a very bad Chance. I muft acquaint you, Sir, the Veffel we came in, is not fo much out of Repair, but that, if you can get Canvas out of the Store for Sails, we can make 'em, and get ready for failing in ten Days Time. And if the Veffel expected here with Supplies comes in a fhorter Time, our Veffel will be ready fix'd for the Ufe of the Governor; and if one Veffel fhould not be large enough to carry us all off, we can go in Company. I imagine you know of the Stores being robb'd, and the Difturbance among the Soldiers, which muft occafion Uneafinefs enough, without repeating Griev-ances, where Relief is not to be had. I beg, Sir, you'll get us difpatch'd with all Expe-dition to his Majefty's Service, that we may not lofe the Opportunity of joining the two Ships and the *Flota*.

S I R, Yours.

The

The next Morning the Lieutenant came down on Horfe-back, being the firft Time of his appearing among us fince we have been here, which is above three Weeks; we went with him to the Commandant, who promifed we fhould not want frefh Beef and Fifh; but as for Bread, there is none to be got. *William Oram*, one of the Carpenter's Crew, died this Day in the Hofpital.

March the 6th, For feveral Days the People very uneafy at the Veffel's not arriving, the Wind having been fair for above three Weeks paft, and little or no Provifions in Store, which makes them doubtful of any to be difpatch'd to their Relief. This Day we are refolv'd to go by Land, if the Governor will only allow us a Guide; we acquainted the Lieutenant with our Refolution; he went with me and Mr. *Jones* to the Governor; we obtain'd Leave to go, with the Promife of a Guide. Captain *P——n*, being at the Governor's, defired to go with us; the Governor told him the Journey was fo difficult and tedious, it would be impoffible for him to encounter with it. The Captain anfwer'd, that he had a Company on Board his Majefty's Ship the *Severn*, where his Duty call'd him, and was determin'd, with the Governor's nor's leave, to fhare his Fate with us by Land; which was granted. The Governor told us, notwithſtanding the preſent Scarcity of Proviſions in the Place, that he had ſo great a Regard for an *Englifhman*, that whilſt he had any thing for himſelf, we ſhould not want; for which we thank'd him heartily. This Governor is certainly a Gentleman of a noble generous Spirit, of exceeding Humanity and Goodnefs; and I believe him to have a ſincere Regard for an *Englifhman*.

March the 9th, This Morning Mr. *Jones* went over with me to the North Side, to make an Agreement for ſix People to go to St. *Catha-rine*'s; while we were here, the Governor received Letters from St. *Catharine*'s, which gave an Account of four Veſſels on their Paſſage for this Port; on the News of this we put by our Journey: It was very lucky we had not ſet out on this Journey before we heard the News: For on the nineteenth the Veſſels from *Rio Janeiro* arrived, and brought an Account that the *Severn* and *Pearl* were ſail'd from thence for the Iſland of *Barbadoes*. Thoſe Veſſels not only brought the Soldiers Proviſions, but alſo a Pardon.

On

On the 20th, The Brigadier arriv'd,
and had all the Soldiers drawn up, where
their Pardon was read to them: He acquainted them with what Money was
come, which was not above a third Part
of their Arrears, but the Remainder was
on the Paſſage. The Money he had for
them ſhould be paid directly, as far as it
would go, if they would take it; but they
cry'd out with one Voice, The Whole or
none, and a great Diſturbance there was;
ſome were for revolting to the King of
Spain, ſome began to change their Notes,
and were for taking Part of the Money,
and the Reſt inſiſted upon the Whole. To
quell this Diſturbance, the Commandant,
whom they look'd upon more than the
Brigadier, or the Governor, uſed his utmoſt
Endeavours. They told the Commandant
they were no longer Soldiers than while
they were in the King's Pay, and let thoſe
who are for the King, draw off one way
by themſelves; you are our Commander,
we truſt in you to anſwer for us, what
you do we will ſtand by with our Lives:
On which the Commandant deliver'd his
Command up, ſhouldering his Firelock, and
took the Place of a common Soldier, telling
them,

them, fince the King was fo good as to pardon them, he thought it his Duty to accept it; the Brigadier was fo well pleafed with the Behaviour of the Commandant, that he ran to him, took him in his Arms, and embraced him; the reft of the Soldiers follow'd the Example of their late Commandant, delivering their refpective Commands up to their proper Officers. This Day put an End to the Difturbance and Confufion which had been fome time among them, and reftor'd them to Tranquillity, good Difcipline, and Order.

March the 22d, This Morning went to the Lieutenant for Leave to go in the firft Veffel, which was expected to fail in four Days time; he told me he expected to go in her himfelf, and that we could not go off all in one Veffel; there might be Room for the Officers, but the People muft wait another Opportunity. I told him that it was a Duty incumbent on the Officers that were in Pay, particularly, to take Care of the People; you, Sir, have been fure of half Pay ever fince the Ship was loft; we are not, but I will tarry myfelf behind with the People, and be anfwerable for them, if you'll give me a Note under your Hand to fecure me the Value of my

Pay, from the Loſs of the Ship; otherwiſe
I don't know any Buſineſs I have but to endeavour to get to *England* as ſoon as I can,
and will put it out of your Power to prevent
my going off in the firſt Veſſel. I left the
Lieutenant, and went with Mr. *Cummins*,
Mr. *Jones*, Mr. *Snow*, Mr. *King*, and Dr.
Oakley to the Governor, to obtain leave
for our going; the Lieutenant follow'd us,
and ſaid, but one half could go at a time.
The Governor told us it was order'd that
the Land Officers, myſelf and the reſt that
apply'd to go by Land, ſhould be the
firſt diſpatch'd and might go on board
when we would; but as the Veſſel did not
belong to the King, we muſt buy Proviſions,
and pay for our Paſſage. I ſaid, Sir, we
have not Money to anſwer the Expence: He
then ask'd me whether I had not ſeveral
Times apply'd to him for Leave to go by
Land at my own Charges? I anſwer'd, we
were obliged to diſpoſe of our Watches to
raiſe that Money, which will barely be ſufficient to carry us ſix off that intended to
go by Land, therefore what muſt become of
the reſt who have not a ſingle Penny? And
I hope, Sir, that you are not unacquainted
that the King of *Great-Britain* allows to all
his

his Subjects, diftrefs'd in this Manner, five
Vintins *per* Day to each Man for Subfiftence.
On my faying this, the Governor call'd the
Commiffary and Major; he walk'd and talk'd
with them afide; then came back again, and
told us the Account was fo fmall, that it was
not worth charging the King of *England* with
it; therefore we muft buy our own Provifions, and pay our Paffage; and as to what
we had received from them, we were welcome; upon which we thank'd them, and
came away. We then confulted with the
Lieutenant, to know what could be done
with the People; and that as the Veffel we
came in was not fit to proceed in any farther,
it was to no Purpofe to leave her there;
therefore we defired his Confent to fell her,
believing the Money fhe would bring, would
be fufficient to carry us all off. To this Propofal the Lieutenant confented. We then
apply'd to the Mafter of the Veffel, to know
what he would have for our Paffage; his De-
mand was forty Shillings *per* Man; of which
we acquainted the Lieutenant, who told us
he could not fee what we could do, and, on
fecond Confideration, would not give his
Confent to fell the Boat; for, when fold, he
did not think fhe would fetch the Money.
Thofe

Thofe Words of the Lieutenant put us all to a Stand, efpecially after he had but now given his Confent to fell her; and in fo fhort Time to declare the Reverfe, was very odd; tho' indeed it did not much furprize us, becaufe this Gentleman was never known to be over ftedfaft to his Word. Seeing no Poffibility of carrying the People off without felling the Boat, I told the Lieutenant, if he left them behind, I could not think but fo many of his Majefty's Subjects were fold; and believ'd he had made a Prefent of the Veffel to the Governor. At this the Lieutenant paus'd for a while; and then faid, he had not Money to carry himfelf off without felling his Coat. I reply'd, there was no Occafion for that, when he had a Gold Watch. The next Morning went to the Lieutenant again about our going off; he acquainted us, that the Brigadier had order'd Things in another Manner; that myfelf, and nine more, being the Perfons defirous of going, fhould be difpatch'd in the firft Veffel, and every Thing found us; that he, the Lieutenant, was to tarry behind with the reft of the People, and to come in the next Veffel, an Eftimate of the Charges being made out; and alfo he told us, he had a fevere Check for

requefting

requefting to go firft himfelf, and offering to leave the People behind.

Sunday, March 28, I embark'd on Board the St. *Catharine*'s Brigantine, with the Carpenter, Boatfwain, the two Mates, the Surgeon of Marines, the Cooper, and fix of the People; the Provifions laid in for us were two Casks of Salt Beef, and ten Alcadoes of *Farina.*

Wednefday the 31ft, We fail'd for *Rio Janeiro,* with the Wind at W. fteer'd S. E. and S. E. by E. until over the Bar; then E. by N. and E. N. E. with a fine Gale, and clear Weather; there is not above two Fathom and half Water on the Bar at High-water; when you are in, it is a fine commodious Harbour for fmall Veffels; it is a low Land, of a fandy Soil: Here is Abundance of fine Cattle; with Frefh-water Fifh, Melons exceeding good, Plenty of Water, and the beft Milk I ever tafted.

Thurfday, April the 8th, Little Wind at S. W. and fair Weather. At Ten this Morning anchor'd before the Town of St. *Sebaftians.* The *Portugueze* Pilots, who have been in *England,* call the Land here the *Ifle of Wight;* and indeed it is very like it, tho' not fo large, being only eight Miles in Length. This is a
very

very fecure Harbour for Shipping; a Stranger may go in or out without any Difficulty. At this Place I was afhore, and think it as delightful and pleafant a Place as ever I faw in *America*; abounding with Fruit, as Oranges, Lemons, Bonano's; alfo with Yamms, Potatoes, Fifh, and Fowl.

Saturday the 10th, Sail'd from St. *Sebaftians*; little Wind at S. W. fteer'd out S. E. between the Ifland and the Main; and at Eight in the Morning, on the *Monday* following, we anchor'd before the City of *Rio Janeiro*.

Tuefday the 13th, This Morning we were all order'd before the Governor. A *Dutch* Surgeon was fent for, who fpoke very good *Englifh*. After an Enquiry into our Misfortunes, the Governor order'd him to be our Conful; telling us, that we fhould have a convenient Houfe, with Firing, and eight Vintins a Man *per* Day Subfiftence-Money: He alfo defir'd we might make no Difturbance among ourfelves; which we promis'd to avoid. A Nobleman went with the Conful to look out for our Habitation; they fix'd on a large magnificent Houfe, fit for a Perfon of Quality. This being the firft Day of our coming afhore, they were pleas'd to order a Dinner

and

and Supper out of Doors, and fent us where we were to eat all together. This was the firft Time of the Boatfwain's eating with the reft of the Officers fince we left *Cheap* Ifland. The Conful was fo kind as to fend us a Table, Benches, Water-pots, and feveral ufeful Things, from his own Houfe; we thought ourfelves very happily feated.

Wednefday the 14th, This Morning the Conful went with the Officers and People to the Treafury for our Money. Mr. *Oakley*, Surgeon of his Majefty's Land Forces, was defired by the Conful to fign for it. The Boatfwain, who now look'd upon himfelf as our Captain, was not a little difpleas'd at this. When the Money was received, the Conful would have given it the Surgeon to pay us; but he excus'd himfelf, telling the Conful the Boatfwain was a troublefome Man, and it might occafion a Difturbance; on which the Conful was fo good as to come and pay it himfelf. Being all together, he told us the Governor had order'd us eight Vintins a Man *per* Day; but at the fame Time had made a Diftinction between the Officers and Seamen; that the Money received was to be paid in the Manner following, *viz.* to the Seamen fix Vintins *per* Man,

C c   and

and the Officers ten. The Reason of this
Diftinction was, that the Seamen could go
to work, and get Money by their Labour;
when the Officers could not, but muſt be
obliged to live entirely on their Allowance.
This Diftinction cauſed great Uneafineſs, the
Boatſwain infifting that the People had a
Right to an equal Share with us. The Officers, willing to make all Things eafy, defir'd
the Conful it might be ſo. The Conful reply'd, the Money ſhould be diſpos'd of according to the Governor's Direction, or not
at all. The Boatſwain then objected againſt
the Cooper, becauſe he was no Officer. The
Conful ſaid, Maſter! I believe the Cooper
to be a very good quiet Man, and I dare ſay
will take it as the Men do; but ſooner than
this be an Objection, I will pay the Money
out of my own Pocket. The Boatſwain then
began at me, abufing me in a very ſcanda-
lous and abominable Manner; ſaying, among
other Things, that the Cooper was got among
the reſt of the Pirates, for ſo he term'd me
and the reſt of the Officers. When the Money was paid, we acquainted the Conful, that
we had, till now, been ſeparated from the
Boatſwain; that he was of ſo perverſe and
turbulent a Temper, and ſo abufive in Speech,
that

that we could not bear with him. The
Boatfwain then chofe to be with the People,
and gave us the Preference of the Fore-
Room, where we defired to be by ourfelves.
There were two Doors to our Room; we
lock'd both of them, and went to take a
Walk in the Country : At our Return in the
Evening, we found the Doors broke open,
and a fmall Sword belonging to me was bro-
ken an Inch off the Point, and the Scabbard
all in Pieces. The Boatfwain had in his
Room an *Irifhman*, whom he fent in on Purpofe to quarrel with us. This *Irifhman* and
Richard Eaft, one of our own People, fell
upon the Cooper and me : *Eaft* chofe to engage with me ; he ftruck me feveral Times ;
he compell'd me to ftand in my own Defence,
and I foon mafter'd him During this Quarrel the Carpenter call'd the Guards ; at Sight
of whom the *Irifhman* made his Efcape. I
defired the Guards to fecure *Eaft* a Prifoner ;
but the Officer told me he could not, unlefs I
would go to Prifon with him. I told him it
was my Defire, and accordingly I went. The
Prifon was in the Governor's Houfe. I had
not been there but a few Minutes before the
Governor fent for me ; he enquired of the
Officer concerning the Difturbance, and or-

der'd

der'd me to my Habitation; but detain'd
Eaſt a Priſoner. When I came home, I found
the Boatſwain, and two Renegadoes with
him, all about the Cooper. On ſeeing me,
he repeated his former abuſive Words. He
made us ſo uneaſy in our Lodging, that, to
prevent Murder, we were oblig'd to lie out
of the Houſe. Next Morning Mr. *Oakley*
and Mr. *Cummins* went to the Conſul; he
came with them to the Houſe, where we
were all ſent for; he told us it was very
ſtrange, that People who had undergone ſo
many Hardſhips and Difficulties, could not
agree lovingly together. We anſwer'd, we
never us'd to meſs together; and ſooner than
we would be with the Boatſwain, we would
make it our Choice to take a Houſe in the
Country at our own Expence. The Boatſwain, on hearing this, fell again into his uſual
Strain of Slander and abuſive Language, cal-
ling us Rogues, Villains, and Pirates. It was
the Governor's firſt Requeſt, that we might
have no Diſturbance among us; yet the Boatſwain hath not ſuffer'd us to have a quiet
Minute ſince we have been here. The Conſul went with us two Miles out of the City,
at a fiſhing Village; where we took a Houſe,
at our own Expence, to pay at the Rate of

ten

ten Shillings *per* Month, there being feven of
us in all, *viz.* myfelf, the Carpenter, Surgeon, the two Mates, the Cooper, and a
Seaman. Here we thought ourfelves fafe
and fecure. The next Day, in the Afternoon, two of the Boatfwain's Friends, which
had lately deferted from his Majefty's Service,
and an *Irifh* Clerk with them, came to pay
us a Vifit. They were fo impertinent, as
not only to enquire into the Reafons of the
Difturbance among ourfelves, but they alfo
inftructed us in our Duty, telling us, they
came from our Commander the Boatfwain,
with Orders to fee my Journal. I told them
the Journal fhould not be a Secret to any
Perfon who could read; but at the fame
Time I would never part with it to be copied
out: They then drank a Glafs of Punch with
us, and left us. This is a Place that a Man
is oblig'd fometimes to fuffer himfelf to be
ufed ill; if he refents all Affronts, he runs a
great Hazard of lofing his Life; for here Ruf-
fians are to be hired at a fmall Expence; and
there is no Place in the World where People
will commit Murder at fo cheap a Rate. Between Nine and Ten at Night, three People
came to our Door; one of which knock'd,
telling us that he was the Perfon that was
with

with me and the Cooper in the Afternoon.
Being apprehensive that they came with no
good Intent, we refus'd opening the Door;
telling them, that it was an improper Season
of the Night, and that we did not know they
had any Business with us; if they had, we
told them to come in the Morning: But they
still insisted upon the Door being open'd;
saying, it would be better to do so, than to
be taken away in three Hours Time. When
they had said this, they went away. We did
not know the Meaning of their Words, but
imagin'd they were gone to bring some Asso-
ciates to beset the House; having nothing to
defend ourselves with, we got over the Back-
Wall of the House, and took to the Country
for Safety: In the Morning apply'd to the
Consul, who remov'd us to a House in the
Midst of the Village; he gave an Account to
the Inhabitants of the Design the Boatswain
had form'd against us, either to compel us to
deliver up the Journal, or to take our Lives;
he therefore desired that the Journal and Pa-
pers might be deposited in the Hands of a
Neighbour there, till the Time of our going
off. The People of the Place offer'd to stand
by us with their Lives, in Opposition to any

Persons

Perfons who fhould attempt to do us an In-
jury.

Sunday the 18th, Early this Morning we
were fent for to the Conful. He faid to us,
Gentlemen, as the Lives of three of you are
in Danger, and I don't know what Villainy
your Boatfwain may be capable of acting, in
Regard to your Peace and Safety; I'll endeavour to get you three on Board a Ship bound
for *Babia* and *Lifbon*; accordingly he went
to the Captain of the Ship, who confented
that we fhould go with him, on thefe Con-
ditions, that the Governor would give us a
Pafs, and that we would work for our Paffage; this we agreed to: After this we requefted the Governor for a Pafs, which he
was fo good as to grant, and is as follows:

Nas Fortaleſas ſedeixem paſſar.

A 30 *Abril, .*1742:

> *Podem paſſar par Portugal em*
> *qualquer Nao que ſelle ofreſer*
> *ſemque che ponha Impedimento*
> *algum Bahia,* 19 *Mayo,* 1742.

*D*IZEM *Joan Bocli, e Joan Cummins,*
    e Joan Menino, Inglezes de Naſao, e Ca-
zados em Inglaterra, em quetem ſuas Mulleres e
Fillios, que ſeudo Officais de Calafate, e Conde-
ſtavel, & Joneiro, de imadas Fragatas Inglezas,
dádo a Coſta de Patagonia, che feſivel a porta-
rem, a Oporto do Rio Grande, donde ſelhedeo
faculdade para paſſarem aeſta Cidade. E como
Naferma do Regimendo de ſon ſoberano Nao
venſem ſoldo, algum deſde otempo, que Nao
Pagau detta Fragata, ſelhes fas prefis a paſſa-
rem a Inglaterra, para poderem tratar de
ſua vida em Compania de ſuas Familias; para
oghe pretendem na Naude Liſenſia paſſar a
Citade da Bahia, para da hi Opoderem farer
para Liſboa, na primera ocaſiao, que che for
poſivell,

poſivell, e ſim deſda Nao podem intentar dito tranſporte.

> *Quaime ſedigne dar che Liſenſia que nas Fortaleſas ſelhe nas ponha Impedimento a ſua Paſſagem, Come e Coſtume aos Nacionaes deċte Reyne.*

> A. R O V E.

The foregoing in *Engliſh* thus.

> *Rio Janeiro Grand.*

From all the Forts let them paſs.

April 30, 1742.

> That they may paſs to *Por-tugal* in any Veſſel that offers itſelf, without any Hindrance whatever, to *Bahia, May* 19, 1742.

*J*O H N *Bocli,* [*Bulkeley*] *John Cummins,* and *John Young,* of the *Engliſh* Nation, and married in *England,* where they have

Wives and Children, the one being an Officer, the other a Carpenter, and the third Cooper of the Ship, being an *Englijh* Frigate, arrived on the Coaſt of *Patagonia*; and at their Arrival in the Great River, *i. e. Rio Grand*, Leave was granted them to come to this City; and as in the Service of his Majeſty, they do not advance any Money, from the Time that they paid off the ſaid Ship, they are obliged to paſs to *England*, that they may be enabled there to ſeek their Livelihood for their reſpective Families: Therefore they deſire that they may paſs in the Licenſe Ship to the City of *Bahia*, that they may from thence go to *Liſbon*, by the firſt Opportunity that ſhall offer; and that without the ſaid Ship they will not be able to perform their intended Deſign.

> Leave is hereby granted them to paſs by the ſaid Ship for *Bahia* ; and we command all the Forts to let them paſs, and not hinder their Paſſage, as is the Cuſtom of the Nation of this Kingdom.
>
> A. R O V E.

The

The following is a Copy of the Sollicitor's
Certificate.

*I*STO *be para que todos fabem que os Sen-
bores Abaixo Nomeados y bem mal afortu-
nados, nefta Cidade de Rio Janeiro fe compor-
tarao com toda aboa Dereyfao nao dando efcan-
dalo Apefoa Alguma e Sao Dignos deque Joda
pefoa pofa os favorefer emoque for de Ajudo
para Sigimento de fua Viagem omais breve pof-
fivel para Huropa.*

> John Bulkeley.
> John Cummins.
> John Young.

Hoje ι *de Mayo de* 1742.

> *A fim que Affiney efte Papel
> Como Procurador Sofil da
> Nafao Britanica.*

> Pedro Henriques Delaed.

In *English* thus.

Thefe Prefents.

BE it known to all Perfons, that the un-
der-figned are in a deplorable Condition in this City of *Rio Janeiro*; who have

behaved

behaved themfelves with Decency and good Decorum, not giving any Scandal to any Perfon whatfoever, and are worthy that all Peoplè may have Compaffion, and fuccour them in forwarding their Voyage with all Expedition to *Europe*.

> *John Bulkeley.*
> *John Cummins.*
> *John Young*

The 1ft of *May*, 1742.

> I have fign'd this Paper as a Sollicitor of the *Britiſh* Nation.

> *Pedro Henriq; Delaed.*

Tuefday, May the 20th, This Evening myfelf, the Carpenter, and Cooper, went on Board the St. *Tubes*, one of the *Brazil* Ships, carrying twenty-eight Guns, *Theophilus Orego Ferrara* Commander, bound for *Bahia* and *Liſbon*. The People left on Shore were,

> *John Jones*, Mafter's Mate
> *John Snow*, ditto
> *Vincent Oakley*, Surgeon

John

John King, Boatſwain
Samuel Steok, Seaman
John Shoreham, ditto
John Pitman, ditto
Job Barns, ditto
Richard Eaſt, ditto
Richard Powell, ditto

Wedneſday the 21ſt, Early this Morning the Captain came on Board; on ſeeing us, he ask'd us, How we came on Board without his Leave? Notwithſtanding he gave Leave to the Conſul for our Paſſage, we ought to have waited on him aſhore. There was on Board the Ship a *Spaniſh* Don, a Paſſenger, who told the Captain no *Engliſhman* ſhould go in the ſame Ship with him; therefore deſired we might be turn'd aſhore; but the Captain inſiſted upon doing what he pleas'd aboard his own Ship, and would not comply with his Requeſt. The *Spaniſh* Don, when we came to converſe with him, was very much mov d with the Relation of our Miſfortunes; and ſaid to us, though our Royal Maſters, the Kings of *England* and *S ain,* are at War, it was not our Fault; that we were now on Board a Neutral Ship belonging to a King who was a Friend to both Nations; that

that he would not look upon us as Enemies, but do us all the Service he could. He extoll'd the Conduct and Bravery of Admiral *Vernon* at *Porto-Bello;* but, above all, applauded him for his Humanity and generous Treatment of his Enemies. He made great Encomiums on the Magnificence of the *British* Fleet, and the Boldness and Intrepidity of the Sailors, ftiling the *English* the *Soldiers of the Sea.* He fupplied us in our Paffage not only with Provifions from his Table, but alfo with Wine and Brandy; and durfng the whole Voyage appear'd fo different from an Enemy, that he took all Opportunities of giving us Proofs of his Generofity and Goodnefs.

Friday the 7th of *May* 1742, This Morning anchor'd before the City of *Bahia,* went on Shoar to the Vice-Roy, fhew'd him the Pafs we had from the Governor of *Rio Janeiro*: He told us the Pafs was to difpatch us to *Lisbon,* and that the firft Ship which fail'd from hence would be the Ship we came in; we petition'd him for Provifions, acquainting him of our Reception at *Rio Grand,* and *Rio Janeiro,* that we had hitherto been fupply'd at the Rate of eight Vintins each Man *per* Day. He refufed fupplying us with any thing; upon which I told him, we we had better been Prifoners to the King of *Spain,* who would allow us Bread and Water, than in a Friend's Country to be ftarv'd. The Captain of the Ship, we came in, hearing the Vice-Roy would not fupply us, was fo kind as to go with us to him, acquainting him how we were provided for at *Rio Janeiro,* and that he would fupply us himfelf, if he would fign an Account to fatisfy the Conful General at *Lisbon,* fo that he might be reimburs'd. The Vice-Roy anfwer'd, he had no Orders concerning the *Englifh,* that he had Letters from the King of *Portugal* his Mafter to fupply the *French,* but had no Orders about any other Nation, and if he gave us any thing, it muft be out of his own Pocket, therefore he would not fupply us; The Captain then told him that we were Officers and Subjects to the King of *England,* and in Diftrefs; that we did not want great Matters, only barely enough to fupport Life, and beg'd that he would allow but four Vintins *per* Day, being but half the Sum hitherto allow'd us. The Captain's Intreaties avail'd nothing, the Vice-Roy continuing as fix'd in his Refolution of giving us no Relief; I don't believe there

ever

ever was a worfe Reprefentative of Royalty
upon the Face of the Earth, than this Vice-
Roy; His Royal Mafter the King of *Portugal* is very well known to have a grateful
Affection for the *Britifh* Nation (nor can
we believe he is fo Frenchify'd as this Vice-
Roy makes him) his Deputy differs greatly
from him, he has given a Proof of his Aver-
fion to the *Englifh*. We think Perfons in
the Diftrefs we were reprefented in to him,
could in no Part of the World, nay in an
Enemy's Country, be treated with more
Barbarity than we were here; We work'd
here for our Victuals, and then could get
but one Meal *per* Day, which was Farina
and Caravances. At this Place we muft
have ftarv'd, if I had not by me fome
Money and a Silver Watch of my own,
which I was oblig'd to turn into Money to
fupport us. I had in Money fourteen Guineas,
which I exchang'd with the Captain who
brought us here) for *Portugueze* Money;
He at the fame time told me it would be hard
upon me to be fo much out of Pocket,
and faid if I would draw a Bill on the Conful General at *Lisbon* for the Sum, as if fupply'd from him, upon the Payment of that
Bill,

Bill, he would return me my fourteen Guineas, accordingly a Bill was drawn up by an *Englifh* Merchant at *Bahia* and fign'd by us, being as follows:

NOS *abaixo afignados Joam Bulkeley, Joam Cummins, & Joam Young Vaffalos de fua Magg de Brittánica El-Rey Jorge Segundo, declaramos que temos recebido. da mam do Snor' Cappam de Mar e Guerra Theodorio Rodrigues de Faria a coanthia de Corenta eloatro Mil e Oito Centos reis em dinheiro decontado comque por varias vezes nos Secorreo para o Noffo Suftento des o dia* 17 *de Mayo proximo paffado athe odia Prezente, por Cuja caridade rogamos a Deos conceda mera faud Born fuccefto e por efte pedimos humildeme te ao Snor' Conf[ul Geral da Mefma Nacao' que Aprenzentado que efte Seja nao' duvide em Mandar Sattis fazer as fobredito fnor' Cappam de Mar e Guerra a refferida coanthia vifto fer expendida em Obra pia e que o Eftado da noffa Mizeria epobreza tre nao' pode pagar e por paffar na Verdade o Refferido e nao' fabermos Efcrever pedimos a Gabriel Prynn homem de Negocio nefta Cidade e Interprete de Ambas as Lingoas*

E e   *ou*

*ou Idofmas que efte por Nos fizefe e Como
Teftemunha Afignafe.*

Sao 44 800 re. *Bahia* 14 *Setembro* 1742.

John Bulkeley.
John Cummins.
John Young.

Como Teftamunha que fiz a rogo dos Sobreditos,
Gabriel Prynn.

The foregoing in *Englifh* thus,

WE the underfign'd *John Bulkeley, John
Cummins,* and *Jahn Young,* Subjects
of his Majefty King *George* the Second, King
of *Great-Britain,* do declare to have received from the Honourable Captain of Sea
and Land, *Theodore Rodriques* of *Faria,*
the Sum of fourty-four-thoufand and eight
hundred *Rees,* in ready and lawful Money,
by different times, for our Support and
Succour from the 17th of *May* Inftant to this
prefent Date : And, for the faid Charity, we
implore the Almighty to grant him Health
and Profperity. And on this Account, we
humbly defire the Conful of the fame Nation,
that, by thefe Prefents, he may not omit
giving full Satisfaction to the above mention'd

tion'd Captain of Sea and Land, for the said Sum, it being employed on a very Charitable Account, being in a deplorable Condition, and not able to repay the Same; And we not knowing in what Manner to write, to acknowledge the above Favours, have defired Mr. *Gabriel Prynn*, a Merchant in this City, and Interpreter of both Languages, that he may act for us; and we leave it to him to do in this Affair as it shall feem meet unto him; and as a Witnefs to this Matter he hath fign'd his Name.

Say 44 100. *Bahia* the 14th *September* 1742.

John Bulkeley,
John Cummins.
John Young.

To the Veracity of the above Affertion I have fign'd my Name,

Gabril Prynn.

Since our being here, we have been inform'd of one of his Majefty's Ships with three Store-Ships being arriv'd at *Rio Janeiro*, fupply'd with Stores and Men for the Relief and Affiftance of the *Severn* and *Pearl*, (which were fail'd before in *January* laft for *Barbadoes)* and that our People were

E e 2 gone

gone on board of them, and 'bound for the *Weſt-Indies.*

Here is a very good Bay for Ships to ride in, with the Wind from the E. S. E. to the Northward and Weſtward back to the S. W. and Wind to the Southward, which blows in, and makes a very great Sea. At the Eaſt Side coming in, ſtandeth *Point de Gloria,* where is a very large Fortification with a Tower in the mid'ſt; from this Point the Land riſes gradually; about a League from hence is the City of *Bahia;* it is ſurrounded with Fortifications and equally capable of defending it againſt any Attempts from the Sea or Land.

Proviſions here of all kinds are, exceſſive dear, eſpecially Fiſh, this we impute to the great Number of Whales that come into this Bay, even where the Ships lye at Anchor; the Whale Boats go off and kill ſometimes ſeven or eight Whales in a Day. The Fleſh of which is cut-up in ſmall Pi ces, then brought to the Market Place, and ſold at the Rate of a Vintin *per* Pound; it looks very much like coarſe Beef, but inferior to it in Taſte. The Whales here are not at all equal in Size to the Whales in *Greenland,* being not larger than the Grampus.

After

After living here above four Months without any Relief from the Governor or the
Inhabitants, who behaved to us as if they
were under a Combination to ſtarve us, we
embark'd on Board the St. *Tubes* with our
good Friend the Captain who brought us
from *Rio Janeiro*; we ſail'd from *Bahia* the
11th of *September* for *Lisbon*, in Company
with one of the King of *Portugal*'s Ships
of War, and two *Eaſt-India* Ships; but the
St. *Tubas* not being able to ſail ſo well as
the other Ships, loſt ſight of them the firſt
Night. About 70 Leagues from the Weſtward
of *Madeira*, we bent a new Foreſail; within
two or three Days afterwards, we had a
very hard Gale of Wind, ſcudding under
the Foreſail, and no Danger happening to the
Ship during this Gale. When the Wind had
ceaſ'd, and we had fair Weather, the Captain,
after the Evening Maſs, made an Oration to
the People, telling them that their Deliverance from Danger in the laſt Gale of
Wind, and that the Ship though leaky making no more Water than before, was owing
to their Prayers to *Nueſtra Senhora Boa
Mortua* and her Interceſſion. That in Gra-
titude they ought to make an Acknowledg-
ment to that Saint for ſtanding their Friend

in

in time of Need. That he himfelf would fhew an Example by giving the new Fore-fail, which was bent to the Yard, to the Saint their Deliverer; accordingly one of the Seamen went forward and mark'd out thefe Words on the Sail, *Deal efta Trinckado pour noftra Senhora Boa mortua* (which is as much as to fay) *I give this Forefail to our Saint the Deliverer from Death.* The Sail and Money collected on this Occafion amounted to upwards of twenty Moydores.

On *Monday* the 23d of *November*, in the Latitude 39: 17: North, and Longitude 6: 00 W. that Day at Noon the Rock of *Lisbon* bearing S. by W. diftant fixteen Leagues; we fteer'd E. S. E to make the Rock before Night. At Four o'Clock it blew a very hard Gale, and right on the Shore; the Ship lay to under a Forefail with her Head to the Southward; at Six it blew a Storm, the Forefail fplitting, oblig'd us to keep her before the Wind, which was running her right on the Shore. The Ship was now given over for loft, the People all fell to Prayers, and cry'd out to their Saints for Deliverance, offering all they had in the World for their Lives; and yet at the fame time neglected all Means to fave themfelves;

they

they left off pumping the Ship, though she
was exceeding leaky. This Sort of Proceed-
ing in time of Extremity is a thing unknown
to our *Englijh* Seamen; in thofe Emergencies
all Hands are employ'd for the Prefervation of
the Ship and People, and, if any of them fall
upon their Knees, 'tis after the Danger is over.
The Carpenter and myfelf could by no'
Means relifh this Behaviour, we begg'd the
People for God's fake to go to the Pumps,
telling them we had a Chance to fave our
Lives, while we kept the Ship above Water,
that we ought not to fuffer the Ship to fink,
while we could keep her free. The Captain
and Officers hearing us preffing them fo
earneftly, left off Prayers, and intreated the
Men to keep the Pumps going, accordingly
we went to pumping, and preferv'd ourfelves and the Ship: In half an Hour afterwards the Wind fhifted to the W. N. W. then
the Ship lay South, which would clear the
Courfe along Shore had the Wind not fhifted;
we muft in an Hour's time have run the Ship
a-fhore. This Deliverance, as well as the
former, was owing to the Interceffion of
Nueftra Senhora Boa Mortua: On this Occafion they collected Fifty Moydores more,
and made this pious Refolution, that, when
the

the Ship arriv'd fafe at *Lisbon*, the Fore-
fail, which was fplit in the laft Gale of Wind,
fhould be carried in Proceffion to the Church
of this grand Saint, and the Captain fhould
there make an Offering equal in Value to
the Forefail, which was reckon'd worth
eighteen Moydores.

On *Saturday* the 28th of *November*, we arrived at *Lifbon*; and on the next Morning
every Perfon who came in the Ship, (excepting the Carpenter, myfelf, and the Cooper)
Officers, Paffengers, the *Spanifh* Don himfelf,
and all the People, Men and Boys, walk'd
bare-footed, with the Fore-fail in Proceffion,
to the Church of *Nueftra Senhora Boa Mortua*; the Weather at that Time being very
cold, and the Church a good Mile diftant
from the Landing-place. We *Englifhmen*,
when we came afhore, went immediately on
the *Change*. I was pretty well known to fome
Gentlemen of the *Englifh* Factory. When I
inform'd them that we were three of the unfortunate People that were caft away in the
Wager, and that we came here in one of the
Brazil Ships, and wanted to embrace the firft
Opportunity of going for *England*; they told
me, that the Lieutenant had been before us;
that he was gone home in the Packet-Boat,
and

and left us a very indifferent Character. I anfwer'd, I believ'd the Lieutenant could give but a very bad Account of himfelf, having kept no Journal, nor made any Remarks fince the Lofs of the Ship, nor perhaps before; that we doubted not but to acquit ourfelves of any falfe Accufations, having with us a Journal, which gave an impartial Relation of all our Proceedings. The Journal was read by feveral Gentlemen of the Factory, who treated us, during our Stay at *Lifbon*, with exceeding Kindnefs and Benevolence.

On the 20th of *December*, we embark'd on Board his Majefty's Ship the *Stirling-Caftle* for *England:* Here we had again the Happinefs of experiencing the Difference between a *Britifh* and a Foreign Ship, particularly in Regard to Cleanlinefs, Accommodation, Diet, and Difcipline. We met with nothing material in our Paffage, and arrived at *Spithead* on the 1ft of *January*, 1742-3. Here we thought of nothing but going afhore immediately to our Families; but were told by the Captain, we muft not ftir out of the Ship till he knew the Pleafure of the L——s of the A———y, having already wrote to them concerning us. This was a very great Affliction to us; and the more fo, becaufe

F f   we

we thought our Troubles at an End. The Carpenter and myfelf were in View of our Habitations; our Families had long given us over for loft; and, on the News of our Safety, our Relatives look'd upon us as Sons, Huſbands, and Fathers, reſtor'd to them in a miraculous Manner. Our being detain'd on Board gave them great Anxiety; we endeavour'd to confole 'em as well as we could; being aſſured, that we had done nothing to offend their L——s; that, if Things were not carried on with that Order and Regularity which is ſtriĉly obferv'd in the Navy, Neceſſity drove us out of the common Road. Our Cafe was fingular: Since the Lofs of the Ship, our chiefeſt Concern was for the Prefervation of our Lives and Liberties; to accomplifh which, we aĉted according to the Diĉtates of Nature, and the beſt of our Underſtanding. In a Fortnight's Time, their L——ps order'd us at Liberty, and we inſtantly went aſhore to our refpeĉtive Habitations, having been abfent from thence about two Years and fix Months.

After we had ſtaid a few Days with our Families, we came to *London*, to pay our Duties to the L——ds of the A——y. We fent in our Journal for their L——ps Infpection:

tion: They had before received a Narrative from the L————t; which Narrative he confeſſes to be a Reſation of ſuch Things as occur'd to his Memory; therefore of Conſequence could not be ſo ſatisfactory as a Journal regularly kept. This Journal lay for ſomeTime in theA—y-O—e; when we were order'd to make an Abſtract by way of Narrative, that it might not be too tedious for their L——ps Peruſal. After the Narrative was examined into, their L——ps, upon our Petition, were pleas'd to fix a Day for examining all the Officers lately belonging to the *Wager.* The Gentlemen, appointed to make Enquiry into the whole Affair, were three Commanders of Ships, Perſons of diſtinguiſh'd Merit and Honour. However, it was afterwards thought proper not to admit us to any Examination, till the Arrival of the Commodore, or elſe Capt. *Cheap.* And it was alſo reſolved, that not a Perſon of us ſhould receive any Wages, or be employ'd in his Majeſty's Service, till everyThing relating to the *Wager* was more plain and conſpicuous. There was no Favour ſhown in this Caſe to one more than another; ſo that every body ſeem'd eaſy with their L——ps Reſolution. All that we have to wiſh for

now is the fafe Arrival of the Commodore
and Captain *Cheap:* We are in Expectation
of foon feeing the former; but of the Captain we have as yet no Account. However,
we hope, when the Commodore fhall arrive,
that the Character he will give of us will be
of Service to us: He was very well acquainted
with the Behaviour of every Officer in his
Squadron, and will certainly give an Account
of them accordingly.

F I N I S.

www.ingramcontent.com/pod-product-compliance
Ingram Content Group UK Ltd.
Pitfield, Milton Keynes, MK11 3LW, UK
UKHW042154280225
455719UK00001B/327